Scouting the Divine

Scouting the Divine

Searching for God in Wine, Wool, and Wild Honey

MARGARET FEINBERG

 ZONDERVAN®

ZONDERVAN

Scouting the Divine
Copyright © 2009 by Margaret Feinberg

Requests for information should be addressed to:
Zondervan, 3900 Sparks Dr. SE, Grand Rapids, Michigan 49546

ISBN 978-0-310-33154-4 (softcover)

ISBN 978-0-310-77339-9 (audio)

ISBN 978-0-310-56402-7 (ebook)

Library of Congress Cataloging-in-Publication Data

Feinberg, Margaret, 1976 –
    Scouting the divine: my search for God in wine, wool, and wild honey /
Margaret Feinberg.
        p. cm.
    Includes bibliographical references (p. 205).
    ISBN 978-0-310-29122-0 (hardcover, printed)
    1. Agriculture in the Bible. 2. Symbolism in the Bible. 3. Agriculture —
Religious aspects — Christianity. I. Title.
    BS680.A37F45   2009
    220.8'63 — dc22   2009029010

Published in association with Yates & Yates, www.yates2.com.

Cover design: connie gabbert | design + illustration

Printed in the United States of America

19 20 21 22 23   LSC   10 9 8 7 6 5 4 3 2 1

Contents

Part II: The Harvest

Part III: The Land of Milk and Honey

Part IV: The Vine

Hidden Bonus Tracks

Wonderment

When Scripture comes alive in our hearts, it doesn't inform us as much as transform us. As I read I'm discovering that faith isn't about becoming good—it's about becoming godly characters in a greater Story. Somehow words on a flat page become the passageway to living encounters with ancient saints and sinners, and with a God who was, and is, and ever will be.

While some dismiss the Bible as a dusty old book, I view its pages as portals to adventure. Not only is the book chock-full of clever plots and compelling stories, but it's laced with historical insights and literary beauty. When I open the Scripture, I imagine myself exploring an ancient kingdom. As I cross the narrow drawbridge into this distant land, I picture a castle with too many banquet halls and bedrooms to count—and enough secret corridors, underground passages, and trapdoors to occupy the most inquisitive visitors for a lifetime.

At every turn I meet kings and queens, scribes and poets, all sharing their stories of courage and faith. With every encounter, I learn something new about their life journeys and am reminded that the Bible is more than a record of the human quest for God: it's the revelation of God's quest for us.

Some of the accounts are downright despicable and shockingly frank in their disclosures: a father offering his daughters to be raped and a woman who nailed a man's head to the floor. Others are simply astounding: men who wrestled with bears and lions, women and children who saved nations, and an unforgettable man who walked from life into death and back again.

The more time I spend in this ancient land, the more I notice that every person's story—even the most unexpected—is a chapter in the greater Story that reveals God's glory as well as his unabashed love for humanity. At times this narrative is clearly displayed in a queen's words or a prophet's proclamation, but I'm slowly beginning to recognize its more subtle inflections—the tone of a raspy voice, eyes dancing wildly with expectation, a long pause before a painful reply. Infused by the Spirit, the chapters enliven my heart, reminding me once again that the Bible is extraordinary. As I read, the Author changes me—reigniting my imagination and rekindling my hope.

Sometimes a single phrase or sentence echoes in my heart long after I close the cover. Other times I discover a passage that seems like it was written just for my particular situation. On occasion I stumble upon transformation.

Yet many days I feel separated from this ancient kingdom by an impassable moat. The accounts are distant and even dull. Though I relentlessly circle the same story a dozen times, I can't find the bridge to the life-giving truths I know are locked inside. I don't connect. I don't understand. In quiet misery, I shut the book, secretly hoping and praying that the next time will be better. Sometimes days roll into weeks and months.

The longing for those spiritual aha! moments has become what I can only describe as a dull ache with occasional shooting pains. You've probably felt them too—those twinklings of yearning to connect with a God who, despite prayer and searching, still seems far away.

Some might say it's all in my head; I think it's all in my heart. Deep inside, I long for the sense of wonderment that comes with knowing God, for those occasions when I wake to find the drawbridge down and the King beckoning me into a castle overflowing with life.

Though I pray for—and try to practice—faithfulness, it's been so long I've started feeling antsy. Lately I've noticed that the day-to-day life described in Scripture is radically different from my own. Though I've lived near farms and ranches, my suburban experience is far removed from the agrarian society of the ancient world. In biblical times, the produce of the land was part of everyday life as a source of food, a sign of wealth, and a foundational element of religious life. Yet my modern world is sharply different. What does it mean to know Jesus is the Good Shepherd and the Lamb of God when the only places I've encountered sheep are petting zoos and Greek restaurants? How do we learn to wait for the harvest when we live in a culture of easy access? How can I understand the promise of a land overflowing with milk and honey when the only honey I buy comes in a bear-shaped bottle at my local grocery store? Can I grasp the urgency of Jesus' invitation to abide in the vine when I shop for grapes at Costco?

The hunger in my heart and mind compelled me to begin scouting the grounds in order to better understand God and his kingdom.

Scouting the Divine tells the story of my attempt to understand some of the nuanced brushstrokes in the portraits of God that I've glanced past all my life. It's an intentional search for ways to move from reading the Bible to entering stories that can be touched, tasted, heard, seen, smelled, and savored. Scripture is sweetness and sweat, bitterness and blood, tremors and tears. Scripture is life—and we are called to live it.

In some ways, aren't we all scouting the divine? Isn't each of us looking for those ordinary and extraordinary moments when God intersects our world?

This story began nearly a decade ago with a shepherd I met in Alaska. My path meandered its way to Nebraska and a farmer's fields before turning west to the residence of a Colorado beekeeper. My latest sojourn was in the vineyards of Napa Valley—though I know this won't be my final stop.

My journey led me alongside people whose experience cultivated my faith. During my time with the shepherd, I watched firsthand as a flock followed its leader with complete trust to new and even frightening places. A farmer reminded me of God's faithfulness and timing. A beekeeper gave me a close-up look at the intricate details of God's creation, while a vintner revealed the meaning of fruitfulness in a way I had never grasped before.

During conversations in warm living rooms and fresh harvested fields, the drawbridge lowered, and the Scriptures opened to me in new and wonderful ways. How does a shepherd understand the twenty-third Psalm? How does a farmer view the last verses of Matthew 9? How does a beekeeper interpret the meaning of a land overflowing with honey? How does a vintner read John 15? Though the practices of agriculture and animal husbandry have changed significantly over the last few thousand years, our conversations still provided gems of spiritual insight and a catalyst for deeper study and reflection.

Your own pilgrimage, like mine, may have already started. My prayer is that you keep walking.

I'll look for you on the road.

Blessings,

Margaret

PART I   The Good Shepherd

1.1 | An Unexpected Encounter

The salmon were in full summer swing in Sitka, Alaska, and I was busy tending my aunt's bed-and-breakfast while she took a much-needed rest. Though the never-ending loads of laundry tempered my romantic notions of life as an innkeeper, I still set the alarm early enough to pick fresh wild salmonberries, blueberries, and raspberries for rainbow-colored scones. By eight o'clock, my treats were out of the oven, cooled only by a firm pat of butter, and paired with freshly roasted Raven's Brew coffee for the guests to savor.

After several weeks, my morning conversations with visitors became rote. Yes, sleeping when the sun is up takes getting used to. It's true: Alaskans consume more ice cream per capita than residents of any other state. The most authentic totem pole carvings can be found at the museum shop, but they aren't cheap—head downtown for the best deals. If you want the chance to see a bear (or salmon or wildflowers) without being joined by two hundred other plastic poncho-wearing tourists, avoid the local park and head out to the end of Halibut Point Road. Oh, and a random piece of trivia you won't find in any of the guidebooks: the house you're staying in used to be owned by televangelists Jim and Tammy Faye Bakker.

That last tidbit always sparked an interest from the guests—mostly retired Americans traveling to a state they promised themselves they would visit decades before they actually arrived.

Lynne and her husband, Tom, had dreamed about a trip to Alaska for years. They were in Sitka to explore the Sheldon Jackson Museum, which boasts one of the best Tlingit cultural displays in the state, along with the famed Russian Orthodox Church filled with breathtaking jeweled icons. The first morning we spoke, I offered a local's perspective on the best Mexican joint for lunch and several off-the-beaten-path nooks worth exploring.

During our second morning together, I asked Lynne what she did with her free time in Oregon.

"I'm a shepherdess," she said.

"Uh . . . what?" I asked, unsure I'd heard correctly.

"I have more than a dozen Shetland sheep that I breed and care for," Lynne replied.

"Where do you keep them?"

"Behind the house," she said matter-of-factly.

Of course, I thought to myself, that's where everyone keeps their sheep.

Lynne explained that they had a fenced-in area behind their Oregon home where the sheep grazed and a barn to keep them safe at night. Intrigued, I began peppering Lynne with questions. All the while I knew what I really wanted to ask her, and since I wasn't sure how to bring it in smoothly, I opted for a quick prayer and a crash landing.

"Do you," I asked awkwardly, "ever read the Bible?"

She looked at me suspiciously. "I've read it before."

"I recently read John 10, where Jesus talks about being the Good Shepherd," I said hesitantly, hoping I wasn't sounding like one of *those* people. "Is it really true that sheep know their shepherd's voice?"

The crash was gentler than I thought: Lynne began sharing tales from her shepherding experience, unknowingly drawing rich parallels between shepherding and God. She explained that when a field becomes barren, sheep are unable to find safe, new ground on their own; they need the careful guidance of their shepherd. And when sheep butt their heads in jealousy and competition, it's the shepherd who restores order and ends the fighting. I found myself hanging on her every word, a spiritual appetite welling inside of me to know more. Alas, morning was pressing toward noon, and Lynne and Tom needed to head to the airport.

"I've been collecting writings that offer a spiritual perspective on sheep," Lynne said. "Would you like me to send you the file?"

"That would be an amazing gift!" I exclaimed, though I suspected it might be one of those well-meaning promises that are never kept.

Late in the afternoon, when my housekeeping chores were finished, I opened my Bible and reread John 10, trying to enter the story with the heart of a shepherd and imagining what the disciples thought as they listened to Jesus. I wondered if I'd ever hear from Lynne again.

Three weeks later, a thick manila folder from Oregon arrived in the mail. As I read through Lynne's collection, I experienced a series of aha! moments. The more I read, the more clearly I understood certain truths of Scripture, but with the passage of time, marriage, and multiple moves, the folder disappeared into my cluttered filing system.

1.2 | Reconnecting

Nearly ten years after I met Lynne, I stumbled upon the manila folder tucked deep in a wooden file drawer of miscellaneous articles and memorabilia at our new home in Colorado. As I flipped through the writings, once again a hunger welled up inside of me. I wanted to live what I was reading. I wanted to sit in a field among sheep. I wanted to watch them interact with each other and their keeper. More than anything, I wanted to shepherd.

I needed to track down Lynne. Getting her contact information was easy—I just typed her name and "sheep" into Google—but would I be able to reconnect with someone I encountered almost a decade earlier?

I picked up the phone. No answer. The message I left was disjointed as I brought up reminders of her visit to Sitka. I expressed an interest in her shepherding, trying not to sound strange—or worse, like a stalker. Hanging up, I whispered a prayer.

Lynne called back later that afternoon. While she clearly remembered her Alaskan adventures, she barely recalled our conversation. "Is there any way I could spend an afternoon with you and your sheep?" I asked, unsure if I was crossing a line.

"I think we could make that happen," she offered hesitantly. "But you should wait until the spring rainy season ends—though I need to warn you that it can always rain in Oregon."

We finally decided the best time for a visit was the weekend after Memorial Day. Lynne and Tom graciously extended their invitation to include an overnight stay in their home. My husband, Leif, and I agreed to bring juicy steaks and gourmet chocolates for dessert.

1.3 | Loving the Flock

Making the final left-hand turn into Lynne's driveway, a gust of panic blew through my chest. Self-doubt tore the roof from my rational mind. *What am I doing?*

I inhaled deeply, hoping to push back the anxiety. Somehow in the preceding weeks I had convinced myself that what I was doing was completely normal. *Of course, I'm going to spend the weekend with a shepherdess I don't really know, who lives in another state!*

Leif looked at me and rested a hand on my knee. "Are you okay?"

"Totally," I said, convincing neither of us. "I'm *totally* fine. I'm *totally* not freaking out."

"You've been looking forward to this," Leif reminded me. "Remember, you love to choose your own adventure."

"Look, the sheep!" I interjected.

Through the car window, we spotted more than a dozen sheep enjoying a lazy afternoon in a wide-open green field. They came in more colors and sizes than I had ever imagined. Their fleeces ranged from basic black-and-white to more complex hues that resembled aged rust and even gray dust. As the gravel driveway narrowed, the opening to the field closed and we found ourselves passing beneath a latticework of trees, branches crisscrossing like fingers folded together. Rounding a bend lined with mossy rocks, we saw a two-story wood home perched next to a stream. We parked near the barn, and a cobalt-blue peacock strutted in front of us.

Lynne and Tom met us in the driveway with an affable greeting, welcoming us inside their home. A sideways glance into the living room revealed the home was decorated with Pacific Northwest nonchalance—a tidy blend of natural wood and subtle shades of ivory, lilac, and cherry.

As I began decompressing from the chest-tightening nervousness I experience whenever I meet new people, I began to notice oodles of sheep everywhere. In our room, miniature sheep carvings decorated a tiny tree atop the television. Wooden sheep rested on top of the dresser and on the floor beside the bed. A shepherd's staff leaned against the corner of the wall. In the bathroom, an acrylic sheep's face sat on the counter, and sheep-shaped soaps (say that five times fast) lay beside the sink—the kind I knew better than to use.

When I mentioned on the phone that I wanted to visit Lynne, she was concerned that I might be better off with someone who raised sheep commercially. But I didn't want to spend time with someone who raised sheep for profit; I wanted a shepherd who loved sheep. Lynne's decor told me I'd chosen well. I had spoken to several people who raised sheep commercially, and they described sheep as more of a nuisance than a delight, a far cry from the love God has for us and that Lynne had for her woolly creatures.

After unpacking, I wandered into the kitchen and found Lynne wiping down the tile counter. The kitchen was part of a great room that included the cooking, dining, and living areas. As I sat behind the counter on an oak stool, I could hear the stream gurgling just steps from the back porch. Spinning wheels, which looked like upside-down wooden unicycles, lined the walls. Lynne must have noticed my interest, which isn't surprising: my face is an open book.

"Spinning was my gateway into shepherding," Lynne explained.

Lynne had enjoyed knitting for many years before deciding she wanted to spin her own yarn. Tom challenged her to go one step further and raise an animal that could provide the raw fiber for her knitting. Starting with a pair of fiber goats, she eventually switched to sheep. She had a special breed in mind, which weren't readily available. Lynne found a farm in Michigan that sold the sought-after-but-hard-to-find Shetland sheep. She ordered three.

"My first sheep were mailed to me sight unseen nearly twenty years ago," Lynne said. "All three sheep were pregnant. Though I had no idea what to do, Rexanna, Cassandra, and Nissa gave birth successfully."

After that first summer, Lynne purchased two rams and her flock continued to grow. "Looking back, I didn't know how to do basic things like trim hooves or give shots, so I had to call the vet for almost anything and everything," she said. "Over time, I picked up new skills. When it's midnight and your sheep is having an abnormal labor and the vet can't make it over, you learn how to get the lamb out. A bunch of years go by, and you end up being sixty-five years old and having a lot of young shepherds calling and asking, 'What do I do?' You wake up one morning and realize you're a shepherd of shepherds."

I smiled. Over the years I've spoken to many pastors who, like Lynne, had grown in their knowledge of God by jumping in and doing what needed to be done. Formal training is great for learning theology and basic leadership skills, but some things you just have to learn by doing. Like Lynne, these pastors experience the triumphs and successes as well as the heartache and isolation that accompany caring for a flock.

"Do you want to go and see the sheep now?" Lynne asked.

I peeked over the counter into the living room. Leif and Tom had slipped into a comfortable conversation on the couch. Encouraged by the go-ahead-we'll-catch-up-later looks from our husbands, Lynne and I headed toward the barn.

1.4 | Sheep, Sheep, Sheep

Pausing by the front door, Lynne pulled a fleece-lined jacket and a pair of heavy boots out of the closet. I grabbed my own coat out of the guest bedroom but noticed Lynne couldn't hide a grimace as I slipped on my hiking boots. I followed her across the driveway toward the barn. She popped open the heavy wooden doors, uncorking the overpowering scents of sweet, fresh-cut hay and heavy, pungent manure.

Lynne pointed out a room on the left. "We just painted this," she announced with a proud smile. "This is our new addition to the barn." She led me to a large window and invited me to check out the view. Through the fingerprint-smudged pane, I could see several pens separated by wood panels, each padded with hay. This window would allow Lynne to keep a closer eye on the ewes during the most critical time of their lives: birthing.

To follow Lynne through the barn was to see her in her element. This was her turf, and her love for the place was contagious. As we walked beside tall stacks of golden hay bales, a large goose poked out its head and honked before swiftly descending to the ground. He circled the floor like he was searching for something.

I traced Lynne's steps through the back door of the barn onto the muddy trail. Lynne marched through the mud without giving the *squish* and *slurp* of the ankle-deep muck a second thought. I looked at my short hiking boots and understood Lynne's grimace. *Bombs away*, I thought, stepping onto the path. The first step was sort of fun, but the second step grounded me in the reality of the situation. On the third step, the soft, wet earth sucked my dainty hiking boot right off. I pushed my heel back down into my boot and felt the cold squishy liquid against my toes. I looked down and realized that the mud wasn't just, *ahem*, water and dirt, if you know what I mean.

"It's best to walk on the broken boards and rocks you can find," Lynne advised without looking back.

I began an odd and precarious dance, leaping on the balls of my feet from rocky outcroppings to cast-aside lumber pieces to avoid the mud-poo. As I progressed with the promenade, I was surprised by how free I began to feel.

I breathed in deep, held the air in my lungs, and tasted the thick, damp Oregon air before exhaling. It was good to be alive. I had been spending too many hours behind a desk and too few imbibing the magnificence of the outdoors.

As we negotiated the narrow path to the upper field, Lynne opened and closed the gates, then double-checked to make sure they were secure before continuing.

"You always have to be careful with gates, because they're crucial to the animals' survival," she said. "Not only do they keep the sheep in—they keep the predators out. The coyotes and the neighborhood dogs are the most dangerous."

I recognized the boundaries as essential to a sheep's survival—and our own. From a sheep's perspective, fences prevent the animal from enjoying greener grass; but from a shepherd's perspective, the boundaries ensure the sheep stays safe and doesn't eat something dangerous or get eaten. Interestingly, in ancient times the flock had to be kept in a stone or wood area overnight and then led to a new field for grazing each day. Shepherds often slept across the openings of their homemade sheepfolds, guarding the animals from predators and thieves with their own bodies. When Jesus describes himself as "the door" of the sheepfold in John 10:9, he is painting a rich portrait of being both protector and provider.

When we crested the hill, Lynne tugged the final gate closed, and we looked out on the expanse of the upper field. Sheep were sprinkled around the muddy pasture like chunks of kosher salt on a giant pretzel. Those closest to us stared while rhythmically chewing fresh grass; those further away remained undisturbed.

"As soon as they hear my voice, they'll come running," Lynne whispered. These were Lynne's sheep. For her, the reality was simple cause and effect.

For me, however, the statement was a paramount moment in my spiritual adventure. *Are the words of Jesus really true?* My throat tightened as a laundry list of *What if*'s clogged my mind. *What if* nothing happens? *What if* the sheep don't respond? *What if . . . ?*

Lynne brought me back to the present. "Sheep, sheep, sheep," she said, her syllables solid and commanding without being threatening.

As the words echoed across the field, sheep began running toward Lynne. A brown, long-haired llama led the way down the path to the lower fields.

What if this is better than I ever imagined? I wondered.

1.5 | Truly Known

"That's Haley, the llama," Lynne explained. "She thinks she's a sheepdog. If there's ever a predator, she lets out a loud shrill to let me and the flock know."

The sheep ran toward Lynne, but she stood firmly, her hand extended toward the trail. Though they responded to Lynne's voice, Haley led the flock down the path. Lynne stood still and alert, her eyes locked on the sheep. "I'm always counting, because you never know when one will remain in the field from sickness or injury."

In one of his parables, Jesus tells of the shepherd who discovers one of his sheep is missing. The shepherd leaves the ninety-nine sheep to scout for the lost one. Upon finding the animal, he throws it over his shoulders, returns home, and joyfully tells all his friends what happened. Though I had read the story many times before, I never realized until that moment that shepherds carefully keep track of their flocks by constantly counting, continually checking.

Before visiting Lynne, I had researched the Bedouin and shepherds of ancient Israel. Whenever I had pictured a shepherd, whether ancient or modern, I always imagined them with a staff in hand. I read that for thousands of years, the staff was an indispensable tool for guiding the flock and defending it from wild animals. Numerous names are given to these long wooden sticks, including rod, stave, crook, and scepter—words which are frequently interchanged in Hebrew Scripture. Yet Lynne didn't have one with her.

"Do you ever use a staff with your sheep?" I asked.

"You probably saw the one I have in the guest room," Lynne said. "I used it a few times, but I discovered that with the size of the Shetlands I don't generally need it, although it's helpful for navigating slippery hills like this one."

As we followed the trail to the lower pasture, Lynne introduced me to particular sheep. "That's Opal," she said, pointing to a silvery ewe. "She's a great mother, though this year she's more possessive of her lamb. Maybe it's because she gave birth to only one instead of two babies, and she lambed later than the rest. She has a weight problem. During her pregnancy, she was so large I honestly thought she was going to have triplets. Her voice is different from any of the others. It's raspy, more of a bleat than a baa-aa.

"This is Iris, and her nickname is 'Herself,'" Lynne added, scratching one of the sheep under the chin. "She is self-confident and goes her own way. If there's an open door, she's the first to be out of it. Iris sure knows how to get into trouble, but on a warm, sunny day, she's also the first to come and lie down beside me."

She pointed to a sheep that looked older than the rest; its dark wool was uneven in length, its face scarred. "The black one, well, that's Meggie," Lynne explained. "She's fourteen—already two years beyond the average life expectancy—and as a granny she'll stomp her foot if she gets mad at you. But make no mistake; she's loving and kind."

One sheep seemed particularly taken with Lynne. She pushed against Lynne's leg in an effort to get additional attention. "That's Jovita; she's just the sweetest. She likes to sit on my lap, and she'll even nibble on my nose. I call her my 'lap sheep.' Dove, who had a difficult pregnancy, abandoned her, but Iris adopted her. Love that Iris. There's a lot of flock drama, you know."

I didn't know, but I was quickly learning. Sheep and people share more in common than I ever dreamed. As we walked, Lynne described each sheep with the same tender attention to detail as a mother. Where I saw a flock of similar sheep, Lynne saw individuals with unique characteristics and quirks. Her affection reminded me of the psalmist who describes every person as being known intimately by God (Psalm 139:13–16). Just as Lynne had a tender history with each of her sheep, each of us has a personal history with the Shepherd.

On the lower pasture, we both squatted on the dirt. At the cry, "Sheep, sheep, sheep," young rams and eager ewes pressed up against Lynne for a handful of the grain she had scooped up on her way through the barn. The flock cautiously warmed up to me, not because of anything I did or said, but for the sole reason that I was near their shepherd.

1.6 | A Tender Ewe

Surrounded by the flock, Lynne showed me how to place my palm up and wiggle my fingers in a beckoning motion. My confidence grew as one of the sheep slowly responded to my invitation. I felt the animal's cool nose against my palm, the springy waves of wool that seemed charged with voltage brushing back and forth with each bite. Feeling one of the sheep's teeth press against my index finger, I became scared. Lynne assured me that as long as I kept my fingers together, I was safe; she wouldn't bite.

As the various sheep grew braver with me, I became more courageous with them. While I made sure one hand was full of grain, I used the other to caress their foreheads and feel their fleeces. I found the contact with the sheep not only soothing to the animals, but also to me.

I noticed a tiny ewe lamb the color of fresh snow. I wanted to cuddle the lovable baby lamb, but its protective mother intentionally kept it away from the other sheep—and us.

"Is that Opal?" I asked.

"Yes!" Lynne said, pleased that I was already able to identify one of her sheep. "She's the protective one guarding Swan."

"May I pet Swan?" I asked.

Lynne leaned against the gate for a moment, looking at Opal with steady eyes. "Not until the mother is ready. Opal doesn't even want me around Swan yet."

1.7 | The Rambunctious One

As the treat supply dwindled, so did the surrounding sheep. Many returned to the edges of the field to graze, but a few remained, each taking a turn to be scratched beneath the chin before moving aside to let another sheep in.

Angry that he wasn't the center of attention, one of the young rams, Alano, began butting me with his horns. The first time was reasonably gentle, but I still gave Alano the stink eye. He stepped back. We locked eyes; he took a few more steps backward, then made a running start toward me. The winsomeness of the moment vanished.

"Lynne!" I cried out.

"You can't let him do that," she said sternly. "Grab him by the horn."

I reached out, clenched my fist around one of his curved horns, and held Alano at arm's length. "No!" I said firmly, as if I was disciplining my dog, Hershey. Foolishly thinking the ram had lost his machismo at the sound of my firm rebuke, I released Alano. He took a few steps back and rammed me again.

"He has to be disciplined now," Lynne said, grabbing the rambunctious ram by the horn. Dragging Alano into another fenced section, she placed him in isolation from the other sheep. Lynne returned to the grass beside me, and together we watched as Alano stood pitifully at the gate, his baa-aa's sounding more like moans.

Alano was one unhappy ram. But if he didn't learn, Lynne's next course of action would be neutering him; a surgery that would transform Alano into what Lynne called "a tame lawn mower."

"If I don't discipline him now, he will grow up to be dangerous and of no use to anyone," Lynne explained. "He's sitting by the gate because he hates being alone. That's why he's crying."

"So that's what a sheep in time-out looks like!"

I had read that some shepherds use time-outs and others use squirt bottles to try to discipline their sheep. If a ram grows up with no fear of its shepherd and no respect for other sheep, the most humane act is to slaughter it. Lynne confirmed this. An unruly ram will hurt or kill others if it isn't destroyed.

"My rams need to respect me and know who I am," Lynne explained. "It's normal for rams to want to bash objects, which is why I give them balls and other toys. But make no mistake, an uncontrollable ram can cause immense damage to a flock. They need to know I am to be respected."

1.8 | Roots

As we reentered Lynne's home, I yanked off my mud-poo-caked hiking boots at the door. The back of my left sock was still damp and caked with the farm's ubiquitous mixture of mud and feces. I excused myself to change and returned to the kitchen where the aroma of sweet basil from ratatouille filled the air. Over a hot bowl of the soup and thick, crusty sandwiches, I learned more about this couple who had once lived a very different life.

Lynne was raised in Boston but spent more than twenty years in Los Angeles working as an executive at a nonprofit. Tom, a pastor's kid, was a psychologist. After the two met and fell in love, they recognized they were working too much and began dreaming of escaping the city for a slower-paced lifestyle. They explored the Pacific Northwest, and Tom discovered the parcel of land they have called home for more than two decades.

"I was the full-fledged city girl," Lynne recalls. "Acrylic nails, expensive haircuts, and spiky heels. I didn't even own a pair of jeans."

I found it hard to believe that this woman in an old sweatshirt and manure-caked boots was once a self-proclaimed valley girl. I also struggled to imagine Tom—clearly so comfortable in their warm, country kitchen—sitting in rush-hour traffic. It seemed that the two of them had found the perfect place.

When I asked Tom about growing up as the son of a pastor, he said that his father seemed more dedicated to being a minister than a dad. The ripple effects were subtle but devastating. A spiritual refugee, Tom was frustrated by the institutional church he'd grown up in.

Once the couple settled in Oregon, Tom reopened his psychology practice. Lynne spent the first few years detoxing from a career that had unintentionally morphed into her identity. Over time she fell in love with a simpler way of life.

One day Lynne and Tom found a stray duck in their backyard. Then they adopted a cat (who was neither fast enough nor smart enough to catch the duck). Then they added a second cat. Over time, they brought in two angora goats and then the Shetland sheep. Before they knew it, they were caring for twenty sheep, fourteen peacocks, six cats, five turkeys, three geese, a llama, a dog, and an assortment of chickens and ducks.

As she grew into her new life, Lynne decided to learn how to play the harp; Tom favored the hammered dulcimer. Together, they took up Spanish as a second language. Lynne returned to work, this time serving the local homeless and poor. Tom and Lynne's jeans, thick sweaters, and muddy boots told the story of their transformation.

"We love to share this place with people," Tom said. "We find that people are more open. Where I work, I describe my office as 'A Safe Place to Talk,' but our home is 'A Safe Place to Be.'"

Something about being on the farm made me extra hungry. I offered to refill everyone's soup bowls and we chatted, enjoying second helpings.

"Our home and these animals, especially the sheep, have connected us with people in a special way," Lynne added. "When you work for the local government, you don't typically mix work and personal life, but almost everyone I work with has either been here or at least talked about sheep with me. I think that's a good thing. Awhile back, I sold a sheep, and I asked the new owner what she did, and she told me about a new nonprofit agency whose mission is to reach out to the homeless. I told her about my work with the county to end homelessness. Because we connected through sheep, we've been able to work together to create new resources for those in need."

1.9 | Fighting for Piaget

Our conversation carried well into the afternoon to the soundtrack of the crackling woodstove. Late in the day, Lynne asked me to help her change one of the sheep's bandages. As we made our way back out to the barn, she told me the story of this special sheep named Piaget (Pee-uh-zhey).

Each spring Lynne sold her lambs to local farms, but one year she found herself one lamb short on the number promised. To make up the difference, she purchased one from a nearby farm. When she picked up Piaget, she looked into the lamb's serene and trusting eyes and thought, I don't know if I can give up this one.

By the time Lynne arrived home, she was flip-flopping on whether or not to sell the ewe, but the buyers were waiting for her in the lower pasture. She took another look at Piaget's face and knew she couldn't let her go. She placed Piaget behind the barn before greeting the expectant buyers and apologized that her ewes hadn't produced enough lambs. The buyers purchased one from another farm instead.

Lynne never regretted her decision.

"Piaget's personality is special," Lynne explained. "She's a good mother. Oh, and her ears are different than the others. Most sheep keep their ears pointed up at full alert, but Piaget's are sideways. She has this way of looking at you with her head slightly tilted. I call it the 'Piaget look.'"

Several weeks before my visit, Lynne noticed that Piaget was the last to come down from the upper pasture. The young ewe had given birth to twins, Miguel and Mario, who immediately took to their mother. Concerned by her slow gait, Lynne watched Piaget closely to make sure she was eating properly. Though she chewed her evening portion of grain, Piaget's behavior was unusual.

When Lynne called the sheep from the upper pasture the next afternoon, Piaget was nowhere to be found. Miguel and Mario were anxious and hesitant, a sign that their mother was ill. Lynne found Piaget resting alone in the middle of the field. Upon seeing Lynne and hearing her voice, Piaget struggled to stand and walk toward her shepherd.

Lynne knew something was wrong. Piaget's temperature was a dangerous 106—four degrees above normal. One side of her udder was hot and hard, with only a small quantity of milk. Plus, she showed no interest in grain or her lambs. Lynne administered nutrients and vitamins and massaged the infected udder.

The next day after work, Lynne came home to a very sick sheep. Piaget wobbled, as spasms shook her weakening body. Lynne managed to find a veterinarian on call who promised to be at the farm within twenty minutes. Sitting beside her dying sheep, Lynne prepared herself for the worst.

The vet confirmed that Piaget was dangerously ill. An infection in her udder was wreaking havoc on her immune system, and she was battling pneumonia. Most shepherds would put down a sheep this sick, but Lynne loved Piaget too much.

"There's a word that I am supposed to use, and that's *cull*," she explained. "Sometimes I have to put a sheep down because it's in pain, but *culling* means getting rid of a sheep because it's too old, imperfectly structured, or its wool isn't good enough. Many farms cull ewes who don't have twins. Culling is not something I do."

For more than three weeks, Lynne placed her life on hold for Piaget. Appointments, Spanish lessons, and deadlines at work all faded into the background as she spent countless hours with the sheep. As a good shepherd, Lynne knew that when a sheep is weak and alone, it is quick to give up.

"I didn't plan to spend this amount of time these past weeks," Lynne said. "But I have learned a lot. I know my sheep and they know me, but this was a different kind of knowing. Because of what we've been through, there's a greater trust between Piaget and me than with the other sheep."

Lynne opened the gate to Piaget's pen. Even if she hadn't been sporting a diaper-like wrap fashioned from an old T-shirt, I would have known this sheep wasn't well. I walked toward her, whispering Piaget's name. She looked at me hesitantly and moved away. Though in a penned area, she managed to stay the same distance away from me no matter which way I turned.

"Piaget."

Lynne spoke her name, and the sheep instantly perked her ears and walked toward her shepherd. Piaget trusted that voice. Kneeling on the ground as she scratched the ewe under the chin, Lynne invited me to come over.

Piaget didn't move. In the presence of her keeper, Piaget knew she was safe. I knelt down beside Lynne and held out my palm. Piaget moved her chin from the shepherd's hand to my own.

Lynne clipped a guide leash onto Piaget's harness and asked me to lead the young sheep to a low-lying table. Lynne and I lifted the bony frame onto the table, securing her head in a padded area designed for her chin.

"You keep holding her head," Lynne instructed.

"You're going to be fine, Piaget," I assured the ewe. "This is going to be over before you know it."

Lynne extracted blood-soaked gauze from Piaget's underside. "I can't tell if it's getting better," Lynne said.

"May I see?" I asked.

The softball-sized fleshy hole was positioned on Piaget's belly, so I needed to get close to the sheep's rear end to get a clear look. From underneath I saw the burgundy wound, pulpy with red, pink, black, and green. The rosy colors meant Piaget was healing; the darker colors were a reminder that she was still fighting gangrene.

I took a photo so we could study the wound on Lynne's computer, taking several shots before I realized something was blurring the lens. At first I thought it was my ring finger. I withdrew my finger, but the fuzzy area remained. I turned the camera over. That's when I saw the runny, soft liquid from a very sick sheep.

"You pooped on my camera, Piaget!"

Lynne apologized, but I assured her that le poop was part of the adventure. I tried my best to comfort Piaget while Lynne filled the wound with fresh gauze, then released Piaget's head. The ewe stepped off the platform, and we led her to the lower field where she grazed at her own pace. Weak and wobbly, she lay down.

"Today's not a good day for her," Lynne said. "I hope the sunshine helps."

"Me too," I said, surprised by how much I cared for an animal I had just met.

On the way back to the larger lower pasture, Lynne grabbed another scoop of grain. Opening the gate, she once again called, "Sheep, sheep, sheep." We sat on the grass as the flock pushed toward us en masse, hoping for a tasty morsel. As the food dwindled, my friend Mario remained. A few others stood by as I scratched each in turn under the chin.

The sun dipped below the fiery horizon, leaving a faint glow of rose and tangerine in the sky. Lynne and I sat in the field with the sheep. At one point, the smallest lamb, Swan, who had watched us all day, dared to break from her mother and head toward Lynne.

The shepherd extended her palm, wiggled her fingers, and spoke the lamb's name. Swan hesitated and then came forward to experience the gentle touch of her shepherd for the first time.

Lynne withdrew her hand. Swan stepped forward, wanting more. With a swift one-armed move, Lynne grabbed the lamb and held her. Swan melted into her shepherd's arms.

"Once they respond to my beckoning, I have them forever," she said as Swan rested her tiny head in the palm of Lynne's hand.

Lynne sounded a lot like Someone I'd been reading about.

1.10 | A Shepherd's Embrace

Swan eventually squirmed, and Lynne released her. Enamored by the lamb, I held out my hand and beckoned the animal. To my happy surprise, Swan moved forward for a scratch. Her silky, soft wool tickled my fingers. Beaming with joy, I stared into her eyes, thrilled by her trust in the tender moment. She returned to her mother, Opal, and I was left with Mario and Miguel vying for my attention. Thankful for the use of two hands, I simultaneously scratched both of them. I read somewhere that petting animals can lower your blood pressure. Maybe it's true. All I know is that I longed for a nap, and I wasn't the only one.

I watched Mario's eyes grow heavy while he nuzzled my hand, until he finally lay down beside me, soon followed by his brother Miguel. As Lynne and I chatted, I was fully aware of Mario's chin resting on my knee and Miguel's warm, soft back pressed into mine.

Seeing that I was sandwiched between two napping rams, Lynne asked, "Do you see what's happened?"

"They feel safe?" I ventured.

"They do feel safe, but that's not all. Look around you," Lynne said.

My eyes scanned the field. I noticed all the lambs were grazing near their mothers. "The families are together except for these two," I said.

"Do you remember why?" Lynne asked.

I shook my head.

"Their mother is Piaget," Lynne said as she plucked a blade of grass and twirled it between her fingers. "Because she's sick and can't be here with us, they've decided that you're their family for tonight."

I thanked God for the delicate moment. I imagined King David as a boy with his own favorite sheep among the flock. He may have given some of the sheep special nicknames based on a personality or physical trait. I can picture David on a hillside with a few of his most beloved sheep napping nearby. Perhaps the shepherd boy allowed his favorite sheep to drink out of his cup—just as I had seen some of the sheep drink out of Lynne's glass as we sat together in the field.

At that moment, I had a greater insight into one of the stories of the Old Testament. I understood why the prophet Nathan's story so enraged the king. After David engages in an adulterous affair with Bathsheba and has her husband, Uriah, murdered, the Lord sends Nathan to tell the king a tale of two men.

Nathan tells King David of a rich man who had huge flocks and herds, and a poor man who had nothing except a little ewe lamb that he purchased, nourished, and adored. Over time, the sheep becomes part of the poor man's family. He shares some of his own bread with the ewe, allowing her to drink from his cup. In the evenings, she falls asleep in his arms. The poor man loves that ewe like a daughter.

One fateful night, the rich man has an unexpected guest he must feed. In his selfishness, he decides not to take from his own flock but from the poor man. He takes the poor man's only ewe, kills it, and serves it to the visitor.

Not until this afternoon with Mario and Miguel did I comprehend the outrage King David must have felt when he first heard this story. Nathan told a God-infused story that stirred holy indignation in David's heart. From his days of shepherding as a boy, David knew what it meant to buy and nourish a lamb, to live for years together, and to share a cup. David knew the soft touch and sweet smell of a baby lamb. He knew the joy that comes with watching an animal fall asleep in your arms. For a rich man to take away the beloved only sheep of a poor man was a heinous crime in this former shepherd's eyes.

Then comes the moment of realization: Nathan is telling this story to expose David's own sin. David is the man who had everything and yet stole from a man who had only one beloved—his wife, Bathsheba. When the truth is framed against his shepherding experience, David finally recognizes the extent of his wickedness.

When David sins, he isn't the only one punished. The child dies. Later on, when he takes a census, the entire flock suffers. The Lord sends a famine to the land of Israel, and the Bible says that seventy thousand died from it. In repentance, David cries out to God, "Behold, it is I who have sinned, and it is I who have done wrong; but these sheep, what have they done? Please let Your hand be against me and against my father's house" (2 Samuel 24:17). David compares the people he ruled over to sheep. He recognizes that his behavior hurt them. David's long days in the fields with the sheep as a child are never far from the shepherd-king's memory.

In the field with Lynne, I relished the time to reflect and think. Already, silence was becoming a friend; the quiet allowed my mind to meander like the nearby stream. Simply sitting idly was something I hadn't practiced in a long while, and twiddling grass between my fingers was more life-giving than I remembered.

Lynne brought me back to reality, reminding me that we still had work to do with the sheep before night fully set in. I followed her as she led the sheep toward the barn. Together, we added fresh hay and replaced the water.

We returned to the house to find Tom setting the table and Leif working on the salad for dinner. They seemed content. We all did. I offered to grill the steaks, and Lynne helped make sure that the bread and side dishes were all ready. As we went about our tasks, we noshed on rice crackers and warm brie, awakening the inner foodie in me. We sat down to a delicious meal and great conversation.

By the time Leif and I crawled into bed, my body was tired, while my mind whirred with anticipation. I snuggled beneath the warmth of a wool blanket and thought about the next day, when I planned to spend some time discussing Scripture with Lynne. I fell asleep dreaming of the Good Shepherd.

1.11 | Woolly Truths

The next morning Leif and I awoke to a soft, rhythmic melody. Lynne was playing her harp, and the notes wafted in and out of the room, along with the scent of applewood-smoked bacon.

When I was preparing to visit Lynne, I created a study I dubbed "Sheep 101." In addition to articles and helpful websites, I read Phillip Keller's *A Shepherd Looks at Psalm 23*. I hunted through Scripture for every place sheep—the most frequently mentioned animal in the Bible—are described. The search for *sheep, shepherd, ewe,* and *lamb* delivered nearly seven hundred references and led me on a variety of side trails, studying predators like lions and bears (oh my!).

Before my in-depth study, shepherds and sheep were merely token characters in a handful of biblical stories—part of the landscape, the lifestyle. Like the animal figurines in my family's Christmas crèche, they could be pushed to the back to make room for more central characters. But as I dug deeper, I began to realize that sheep are integral to the stories of God. The early church even embraced the shepherd as one of its primary images.

Sheep graze throughout the pages of the Bible, beginning in Genesis. Though sheep are not specifically mentioned in the account of creation, God made these animals a valuable source of food and clothing. Because of their worth, contention soon came. The original bloody conflict between brothers Cain and Abel is over an offering; Abel's acceptable gift from the flock versus Cain's rejected gift from the field. The split between Lot and Abram is also sheep-related, as the duo discovers the land can't sustain both of their flocks.

Sheep were also used to garner goodwill. When Pharaoh wants to win favor with Abram, he gives him sheep, among other gifts. Sheep were not only used to reconcile human relationships, but also our relationship with God. Remember that heart-stopping moment when God asks Abraham to raise his knife on his own son, Isaac, as a sacrifice? In Canaanite culture, the fertility god of the day could demand a portion of the bounty of the land in sacrifice—including animals, grain, and even human life. So the request from God was shocking to Abraham, but not nearly as flabbergasting as it would be to us today. Abraham is clearly distraught by the request, and, as he begins to obey, is relieved when an angel commands him to stop. Moments later, Abraham discovers a ram trapped in a nearby thicket. The ram becomes a substitute offering, a symbolic foretelling of the Messiah who is to come. Abraham memorializes the place as "The Lord Will Provide."

Sheep continue their prominence when the Israelites are enslaved in Egypt, many generations after Joseph's time. After the story of the exodus begins, Moses goes on the run because he killed an Egyptian in anger. Settling in the land of Midian, he sees another injustice: the daughters of the local priest struggling to water their flocks because of pushy shepherds. Moses helps them and is taken in by the family—marrying one of the daughters and becoming the very thing the Egyptians who raised him despised: a shepherd. Yet while pasturing a flock, God appears to Moses in flames of fire in the midst of a bush and calls him to set the Israelites free. When Moses protests that the people won't believe him, God instructs Moses to use the staff in his hand to convince them, a sign that Moses would become a shepherd over God's people.

Through a wild series of miracles, Pharaoh grants Moses' demand. God's people are set free but are not permitted to take their flocks or herds. Though the Egyptians detest the shepherds, they obviously know the value of their sheep. Moses refuses to leave without the sheep, and when the Israelites enter the Promised Land, their flocks are with them.

Why is that so important? Because on their way out of slavery, the Israelites are commanded to eat for the first time what would become a powerful institution for God's people: the Passover, which included taking a one-year-old male lamb without defect, draining its blood, and placing the blood on the doorposts of the home; then roasting the meat and eating it with bitter herbs and bread made without yeast.

The inhabitants of those houses marked by the blood are spared from death and loss on that fateful evening when God passes by. The meal is meant to remind God's people for generations to come of his love for them—even for those who did not directly participate in the exodus from Egypt—as well as to create a powerful foretelling of the Lamb of God who would one day die for the sins of the world.

Many of the prophets, including Hosea, Jeremiah, Ezekiel, Micah, Nahum, and Zechariah, use shepherd imagery. Even Amos, one of the most offbeat guys in the Bible, is a shepherd-turned-prophet.

Waiting for the Messiah, the people eagerly anticipated the one who would "shepherd" Israel. This Promised One is Jesus, the Son of God, the Good Shepherd.

Given the importance of sheep and shepherds like Moses and David in the Old Testament, it should be no wonder that shepherds are an integral part of the account of Jesus' birth and life. Upon seeing his cousin, John the Baptist declares, "Behold, the Lamb of God!" Throughout his teaching, Jesus refers to shepherds and sheep regularly in ways the people understand. In their writings, Paul and Peter speak of these animals and the tender care of them. Imprisoned on the island of Patmos, John continually mentions the Lamb he keeps seeing in his apocalyptic visions.

From Genesis to Revelation, the woolly theme blankets Scripture.

1.12 | The Best

Absorbing the warmth of the fire, the four of us sat next to the woodstove and enjoyed the diverse flavors of breakfast and casual conversation. Tom and Leif graciously offered to put away the leftover scrambled eggs, crispy bacon, and poppy seed bagels, leaving Lynne and me to talk.

As my hands cupped a second mug of coffee, more than a few questions swirled around my mind. Rocking back and forth in my chair, I explained to Lynne that I wanted to look at passages of the Bible together.

She seemed hesitant, worried that I wanted theological answers. Lynne made it clear that she could not provide them. I assured her that all the insight I wanted was the honest response from the watchful eye of a shepherd, the perspective of a woman who loved her sheep. Anything she could draw from her years growing up in the church was simply a bonus, and I promised to check in with the theologians later.

Some of the hardest teachings for me to wrap my mind around are the details in the Torah regarding sheep. God makes it clear in Exodus 34:19 that the first offspring "from every womb" belongs to him. In Leviticus 22:27, the instructions become more specific, "When an ox or a sheep or a goat is born, it shall remain seven days with its mother, and from the eighth day on it shall be accepted as a sacrifice of an offering by fire to the LORD."

I asked Lynne why she thought God wanted the first offspring.

"I don't want to even guess about all of God's intentions, but every spring those of us within the shepherding community get excited about our lambs," Lynne replied. "We can hardly wait for the first lamb to be born—especially those of our new moms. All the shepherds talk about it. When the first one comes, it's extra special. It means spring is here, and it's a symbol of new life and hope and joy for us. I think that in the action of giving over the first, you're saying to God that he is first in your life."

I was intrigued by Lynne's experiences with newborn lambs and asked her why she thought God requires that the sheep stay with its mother for a full week before being offered as a sacrifice.

Lynne sipped her coffee for a few moments before answering. "If you take a baby lamb away after the first week, it's hard on the mother; but if you take away a lamb at birth, then it would be terrible. Chemicals, including oxytocin, are released at birth; and there's a special chemical bonding that goes on between the mother and her lamb that first week—especially the first few days. And the udder is full of milk. Natural things God designed are in process that, if interrupted, could jeopardize the health of the mother."

"That's why Opal was so protective of Swan," I said.

"Exactly!"

The image of a lamb bonding with its mother reminded me of a friend who struggled for words to describe those precious first moments of holding her child. She said it was like time stood still, yet she knew she was holding the future in her arms. Lynne was describing a similar mysterious connection that exists between a ewe and her lamb.

I then asked whether it was hard to breed sheep without any spots or blemishes or deformity, since throughout the Torah, God makes it clear that the sheep used as offerings must be perfect.

Lynne explained that if shepherds are careful with their breeding plan, lambs will be produced with the finest fleece. The best fleece is consistent from head to tail. It features rich, lustrous colors, without scattered patches of coarse wool or unwanted spots. This is the wool that is most desired for fine garments.

Every shepherd wants to minimize defects. That's why a good shepherd examines the ewes to make sure they're developing properly. Lynne checks her rams to see if their testicles descend, because that may be a sign of reproductive problems later on. She also examines their legs for strength and straightness, which increases the chances of healthy breeding.

"And you're always looking at the teeth," she explained. "You don't want sheep to have an overbite or an underbite, because that may affect their ability to consume the nutrients they need. All the defects center on a sheep's ability to survive and produce other sheep. The goal is for a sheep to be strong, sustain itself, and create many offspring."

As Lynne spoke, Tom slipped out of the house and returned with an armful of split hardwood. Without a word, Lynne grabbed two of the larger pieces and slid them in the stove to make sure the fire kept us toasty.

"When God is asking for a sheep without blemish or deformity, he's again asking for our best," Lynne said.

"But what's the best?" I asked.

"Like fine art, that's always subjective; yet in every community, including the sheep community, we have standards. When you list God's standards for a sacrificial sheep, you're describing the best of the flock—the one with the finest fleece that will produce the strongest offspring—and that takes years to produce."

Up until that moment, I had never recognized the rich symbolism behind sacrifice. I knew that the spotless sheep was representative of the flawless sacrifice—the Son of God—who was to come. But when God asked for the sheep without blemish, spot, or defect, he was asking the people not just to hand over their best, but also to sacrifice something they had worked years to develop.

I imagined shepherds struggling, season after season and year after year, to create what was, in essence, the perfect sheep. Then they sacrificed the animal. For me, it would be like spending months working on the perfect prose, then lighting a match and burning it. The act places me in a posture of depending on God to create through me again. For the common shepherd, sacrifice meant trusting that another strong, perfect sheep would come along and contribute to the flock's long-term survival. I now understood why the temptation to hold back or offer a less-than-perfect sheep at the altar was so great.

And God didn't just ask for the perfect sheep; he also wanted its wool. Deuteronomy 18:4 instructs shepherds to give the first shearing of the sheep as an offering to God. Above the crackling warmth radiating from the stove, I read the verse aloud to Lynne.

"Is a first shearing a once-in-a-lifetime offering?" I asked.

"Yes, everybody wants the first shearing, especially if it's from one of your best lambs. The first shearing is the finest fleece that's used for the best clothes. First fleece is the wool that's neither itchy nor scratchy, the wool everyone wants next to their skin. It's also the smallest shearing, because of the size of the sheep. To ask for that is a real sacrifice!"

That meant each sheep's best wool comes only from its first-ever haircut, with every subsequent shearing decreasing in value. I was intrigued by the idea that God asked for the first virgin wool, a shearing that could never be recovered. I thought of the soft wool blanket I had nestled underneath the previous night. "Was that first-shearing wool?" I asked.

Lynne nodded and invited me to follow her up the thick wooden stairs to the second floor. Through the window, I noted the cloudy skies were unleashing a misty rain. The stream beside the property had quickened. A handful of ducks stood on the bank, seemingly unsure whether it was safe to dive in. Turning my attention back indoors, I watched Lynne pull open two slatted wooden closet doors to reveal wool bagged like fluffy cotton candy. The delightful softness came in unexpected colors—green apple, bright tangerine, fresh pomegranate. Each bag was tagged with a white sticker. Black Sharpie markings revealed the sheep's name and the date of the shearing.

"Those are some of the fun colors I've tried in the dyeing process," Lynne said. "But look at these."

She reached into a drawer and pulled out two bags that boasted more natural, earthy colors. The wool samples were from the same sheep, Jovita, but they were taken years apart. Lynne invited me to feel the difference between the two.

I reached for the thicker gray clump first. Though matted, with curlicues of amber sprinkled throughout, the wool was pleasant to touch. I could feel a few strands of dried grass in the wool, a reminder that the shearing had not been processed.

Lynne handed me the second bag, which held charcoal-black wool from Jovita's first shearing. I pressed my forefinger and thumb together and felt the delicate, velvety texture that now made the first bag of wool seem scratchy. I reached back toward the gray wool to confirm for myself what Lynne already knew: there was no comparison.

For the first time in a long while, maybe ever, I had felt with my own hands what God desired from sacrifice. It was nothing like what I expected. All too often when I think about giving my best to God, I think about giving big. But in asking for the first fleece, God isn't asking for the biggest. He wants the smallest and softest.

He doesn't want more—he wants the best.

1.13 | Dependence

We returned downstairs to coffee refills and vibrant discussion. One of the references that caught my attention was a word picture used throughout the Old and New Testaments. Concerned about who would lead God's people after his death, Moses petitions God: "May the LORD, the God of the spirits of all flesh, appoint a man over the congregation, who will go out and come in before them, and who will lead them out and bring them in, so that the congregation of the LORD will not be like sheep which have no shepherd" (Numbers 27:16–17).

I read the passage aloud to Lynne and explained that this image is not only used by the prophets but also in the Gospels to describe what Jesus saw as he looked out on the crowds.

"Lynne, what happens to sheep without a shepherd?" I asked. "What would happen if you went away—even for a few weeks— and left your sheep without anyone to care for them?"

From across the kitchen, Tom raised his eyes above the edge of the newspaper he'd been perusing. "They'd be dead," he said with conviction.

"Lynne has a friend who had one of her Shetlands escape," Tom explained. "The sheep went off into the woods. We don't actually know what happened, but we have a pretty good idea."

The silence following Tom's response lingered, and I imagined the fate of that sheep. I pictured the woolly creature feasting on grass that was once off-limits, a scene that had repeated itself in many forms since the original forbidden fruit was eaten in the garden. Each bite of the grass tasted better than the previous one. Maybe the sheep wandered toward deeper, more tempting sections of the forest. Unbeknownst to the animal, two beady eyes were watching its every move. The predator ran its tongue along razor-sharp teeth.

Almost reading my mind, Lynne awoke me from the spell of my

daydream. "It's not just predators like coyotes," she said. "Parasites and poisonous plants can also kill a healthy sheep. But probably the greatest threat is too much good food. Sheep often kill themselves by upsetting the delicate balance of their rumen by eating too much grain or rich new green grass. Once the balance of their rumen is upset, they will die within a few days if left untreated."

While too much food threatened Lynne's flocks, I knew from research and travel that the shepherds of the Middle East faced a different challenge. Israel is far different from Oregon. A wandering sheep won't accidentally find itself in knee-deep alfalfa or supple grass. In fact, watching most sheep in Israel, one would think they were rock-eating animals. Their heads may be down, but from a distance there's little hint of vegetative life. The local shepherds know which hillsides will sprout new slivers of grass overnight, and they lead their flocks there to graze. The sheep are literally dependent on their shepherd for their next mouthful. Interestingly, when Jesus teaches his disciples to pray, he instructs them to ask God for daily bread, not yearly or lifelong bread—a reminder that, like a shepherd, God leads us every step of the way.

I noticed that Tom had placed his newspaper on his lap and was watching us intently. "Tom, what kind of odds for survival do you give a sheep without a shepherd?"

"Zero."

"But there's always a chance," I protested.

"Then whatever is closest to zero," he conceded.

I looked to Lynne for some sign that Tom was wrong, but she nodded in agreement. Her compassionate, light-brown eyes affirmed this bad news: sheep are mutton on a stick without a shepherd. "Distressed and dispirited like sheep without a shepherd," this is how Jesus saw the crowds who followed him. My thoughts rested on this passage as my eyes caught Lynne's; a new depth to this truth was opening up before me as I glimpsed what Jesus saw and felt.

When Jesus looked out on the crowds that day—hot, sweaty, pressed up against each other on the rocky mountainside, grateful for any rock or patch of grass offering rest—he didn't just see a group of people. He saw defenseless individuals of incredible worth who needed his help.

Sheep are defenseless against more than just predators; they also have to be rescued from what seem like more benign predicaments. For example, when a sheep rests in a hole and rolls onto its back, the weight of its fleece can cause it to die without a shepherd to flip the animal back over. When a sheep's fleece gets so heavy that it becomes a painful burden, it needs to be shorn. When sheep butt heads in competition, the shepherd is the only one who can restore order. And only a shepherd can bring comfort when the sheep grow anxious, agitated, and afraid.

Without someone to protect, guard, and lead us, we are sheep without a shepherd, defenseless creatures who can destroy ourselves or be destroyed with equal ease.

"So sheep need a shepherd because they are dumb and make lots of bad decisions," I clarified.

Lynne's expression morphed into something grim, and I knew I had hit a nerve. She looked at me intently, her eyes penetrating, her voice firm. "Sheep are not dumb," she said. "That may be one of the greatest mistruths about sheep. They are not dumb; they're defenseless. There's a big difference."

"What do you mean?" I asked. "You mentioned that sheep will freely wander into harm's way if given the chance."

"From the outside, a lot of sheep's behavior looks dumb," Lynne replied. "And it's true that they aren't always aware of the consequences of what they're doing, but to describe all their behavior as dumb is a broad generalization."

She explained that whenever there's a predator nearby, Haley, the llama, will make sure the sheep are made aware. But the sheep already know. They gather tightly together as a flock because it's the only thing they can do to protect themselves.

Sheep also trust each other immensely and, in extreme cases, have been known to follow each other right off of a cliff. Partly, this is due to the fact that sheep travel in a straight line, which creates issues when a shepherd calls to sheep across a ditch or hillside. To prevent the sheep from getting hurt, shepherds will guide their sheep in zig-zag patterns down the side of hills. The Hebrew word for "straight" (*yashar*) can also mean "right" or "upright." The Israelites recognized that the path of righteousness is the one that leads straight to the shepherd. Yet despite this awareness of how important it is to stay on the right(eous) path, I'm amazed by my own propensity to wander.

What Lynne said uncovered a subtle yet significant truth. It's all too easy to look at followers of Jesus and bemoan our dumb behavior. Like those two grumpy guys from *The Muppets*, Statler and Waldorf, I love laughing at ridiculous behavior—even my own. When under pressure at work and in my personal life, my own tendency is to freeze. Most people don't see it, because I'm what Leif describes as "bouncy." Yet I shut down to new possibilities, options, and even the most basic decisions. I'll push off opportunities with arguments like, "This isn't the best time," "We can't possibly make this work," and "I can only do so much." Often it will seem like I'm aloof, unwilling to commit, or refusing to take things seriously. But the honest truth is that pressure paralyzes me, and my survival mechanism is to shut down everything I possibly can. Some might call this dumb, but the heart of it all is that I feel defenseless.

Lynne leaned forward in her chair, pressing her palms against the smooth armrests.

"Need a break?" I asked as she stood up and walked over to the truffles I'd brought, popping one in her mouth.

"Actually, I need a snack," she said, flashing a rueful smile. "It's always a good time for a truffle, don't you think?"

I liked this woman.

Within a few minutes, I heard the high-pitched whistle that signaled the hot water for tea was ready. The warmth on my fingertips from clasping the mug softened the edges of the chocolate with each bite. I found myself licking the chocolaty, nougat-like goo from my fingers. Lynne caught me, and my face turned a deep shade of red.

Popping another treat in her mouth, she gracefully mimicked my finger licking, complete with a smacking sound, and then declared these were the best truffles she'd ever eaten.

Now I *really* liked this woman.

1.14 | The Shepherd Boy

As we finished our tea and truffles, I took Lynne to the book of 1 Samuel. I explained that the first mention of someone in

Scripture often reveals something significant about the person's character. The first king of Israel, Saul, is introduced as a young man trying, unsuccessfully, to find his father's donkeys. This humorous scene hints at Saul's later inability to lead others well. Though his early years of ruling God's people are marked by humility and self-control, over time Saul becomes disobedient, jealous, and full of hatred. He's known as the foolish king who lost his crown.

The introduction of Saul stands in sharp contrast to the first mention of David, the second king of Israel. The prophet Samuel is told by God that one of the sons of Jesse will be the next king. Noting that the Lord hasn't chosen any of the first seven sons of Jesse, Samuel asks the father if he has any other sons. Jesse responds, "There remains yet the youngest, and behold, he is tending the sheep" (1 Samuel 16:11). When we meet David, he's watching over his family's livelihood.

The Hebrew word for youngest, *qatan*, implies insignificant and unimportant. One translator even uses the word "runt." Though David is the runt of the litter, God selects him to rule over Israel.

"Does it surprise you that the youngest child was caring for the sheep?"

"Not at all," Lynne said. "In ancient societies, and even today in remote areas, the weakest members of a family are often the ones assigned to care for the sheep. When we were in Peru staying with a family, a five-year-old boy, a few women, and an old man took care of the family's sheep. The shepherds were those who lacked the strength or skill to do more physically demanding labor."

In the Bible, the younger siblings are often responsible for shepherding, while the older children are given more important jobs. Though Cain is older, Abel keeps the animals. While some shepherds were strong like Abraham's son, Isaac, who makes the Philistines jealous with his abundant flocks, many times the younger brothers or even daughters cared for the sheep. Rachel, the younger sister of Leah, is recognized as a shepherdess. In fact, while watering sheep at a well, she meets Jacob and eventually falls in love.

Lynne held up her index finger, signaling me to wait, and disappeared into the downstairs guest bedroom. When she returned, she handed me a brightly colored wool satchel that felt scratchy to the touch. Looking inside, I realized from the imperfect stitching that the entire piece was handmade.

Lynne explained that this was a gift from a shepherd in Peru. In the remote area she visited, the children, women, and elderly shepherds packed a single bag with "survival gear"—portions of food, a knife for protection, an extra layer of clothing, and so on.

I couldn't believe what Lynne was saying. Those considered the weakest members of society—the children, women, and the elderly—were sent out to protect the sheep. In some cases, they're entrusted with the livelihood of the entire family. And they have to do it with such basic provisions! I imagined my grandma beating off a pack of wolves with a stick.

Within this context, the story of David made more sense to me. David isn't just the youngest brother; he's the least qualified choice in the eyes of everyone. He takes care of the sheep, because everyone else in the family has more important duties. Samuel's selection of David must have shocked them all.

Sitting straight up in her chair, Lynne was suddenly on alert.

"Do you hear that?" she asked.

I didn't hear a thing.

"It's Haley!" Lynne said. Before I knew what was happening, Lynne dashed out of the kitchen, threw on her boots, and ran through the light rain toward the upper field. I grabbed my coat and tried to follow behind her. Halfway up the muddy trail, I met Lynne on her way back down.

Slightly out of breath, Lynne explained that the sheep were fine. But the sound she heard was the llama's warning that a predator was nearby. "You develop an ear," Lynne said.

I had a lot to learn about shepherding.

I was intrigued by what had just happened. Lynne had heard a warning cry and took action without hesitation. The reaction was not just one of a good shepherd but also a good leader.

David had been throwing stones his whole life to protect and guide his sheep. Even today, shepherds will throw stones ahead of the sheep to create a clatter that warns the sheep where not to go. As a shepherd boy, David had been schooled in warding off predators, and while still a boy he protected his people using a shepherd's trick—five smooth stones and a slingshot brought down the giant Goliath. How had his time in the field with the sheep prepared him to be one of the greatest kings in the history of Israel? How does shepherding develop leadership skills?

"I think shepherding teaches you a lot about management," Lynne said. "It helps you develop a big-picture perspective and planning skills. In caring for lambs, there are certain things you have to do like weaning, microchipping, and training for a halter. All of these require planning and preparation.

"As a shepherd, I'm constantly scanning when I'm with the sheep, looking for weakness, sickness, and changes in behavior—which teaches you to pay attention to a lot of different things. Caring for a big flock multiplies the need for all those skills, including learning to anticipate, schedule, organize, and strategize.

"Shepherding also teaches you how to lead from the front rather than the back. Whenever sheep are pushed, they'll respond in fear or anxiety—even when, as their shepherd, I do it. Pushing a sheep produces agitation. But when I go ahead of the flock and call them by name, they follow me peacefully. They trust me, and they want to follow. Anyone can lead by agitating, but leading in such a way that those behind you want to follow is an art form."

Lynne's words echoed some of the wisdom of the Psalms. In Psalm 78:72, we learn that David shepherds with integrity of heart, and with skillful hands he leads his sheep.

Noon was approaching, and our time with Tom and Lynne was running out. Our flight was leaving mid-afternoon, yet some of the most intriguing Scriptures about shepherding remained unexplored. I had long been familiar with the miraculous events surrounding the story of Jesus' birth, but time with Lynne and her flock suddenly gave the story renewed, almost urgent, significance. Opening my Bible, I read the portion of Luke 2 which described the shepherds living out in the fields watching their flocks in the night. I imagined the shock on their faces when angels illuminated the lonesome darkness with their divine message.

Reflecting on all I had learned from Lynne, I recognized something new in the passage; namely, the shepherds probably weren't the male figurines I moved around in the crèche as a child. The shepherds included in the birth of Christ were most likely children, women, and perhaps, the elderly.

Pausing for a moment, I meditated on our bighearted God—a God who in his tender love sent a host of angels to ensure that those who are often marginalized in our world were invited to witness the greatest moment in history alongside the kings and wise men. I also recognized a new facet of what Jesus was saying when he called himself "the good shepherd." On one level he was intentionally associating himself with the marginalized and outcast. Neither he nor his father played it safe in their titles— using only *king* or *redeemer*—but they reached out to the young, the weak, and the old by embracing the name *shepherd*.

I read, "Behold, I send you out as sheep in the midst of wolves; so be shrewd as serpents and innocent as doves" (Matthew 10:16).

"Does this mean that God wants his children to be like helpless sheep in the midst of predators? What does that mean to you?" I asked Lynne.

"When the sheep are in the pasture and a predator like a dog walks by, and they're in danger or what they perceive as danger, the sheep are alert!" Lynne explained. "They will come together as a group. To me, that's being shrewd. If you're a sheep in the midst of wolves, you're not going to stand alone, chew your cud, and wait for a wily wolf to jump you. You're going to do everything possible in being alert, bold, and together."

"How does that affect the way we act and react?" I pressed.

"I think Jesus is saying you need to be vigilant, alert, and even stomp your foot like sheep do in boldness, but in the end never give up being a sheep," Lynne said. "Never give up your sweet, trusting nature. Always remember the strength and safety that comes in community."

I know many people who have left the safety and protection of the flock of the church to pursue God on their own. I applaud their desire for an authentic relationship with Jesus, but I wonder if a parallel exists between the safety found in a flock under the care of a good shepherd and the safety found in a church under the care of a good pastor. Some of my friends who quit the church have had their belief systems infected by parasites of bitterness and anger or have been unable to heal. Others have been picked off by predators of doubt and quit believing in God altogether. Still others have held on, searching for sustenance and fellowship with other wandering sheep. Yet those who choose such a path often find the journey far more difficult and perilous than they ever imagined.

1.15 | Bad Shepherd

While I felt a deep admiration for Lynne's warmhearted shepherding, I had to remind myself that not every shepherd was as caring or kind to their animals. Jesus refers to himself twice as the Good Shepherd, but the existence of good shepherds implies bad shepherds too. Many of the Old Testament prophets allude to bad shepherds in their writings.

In Ezekiel 34, the prophet rebukes Israel's shepherds as those who were feasting on their flocks rather than guarding them. Employing rich imagery, the chapter describes the bad shepherds leaving sick, diseased, and injured sheep in distress and allowing the flock to fall to predators. Rather than leading with love and gentleness, the Scripture says, "With force and with severity you have dominated them" (Ezekiel 34:4). The passage goes on to describe God stepping in as the Good Shepherd to gather the scattered flock and lead it to restful pastures.

In the New Testament, Jesus intentionally draws on this contrast between good and bad shepherds when he references the Ezekiel passage in his encounter with Zaccheus (Luke 19). A man of short stature, Zaccheus could have pressed his way to the front of the crowd to see the teacher everyone had been talking about. But he decided his best chance to see the traveling rabbi was to climb a tree.

Everyone is shocked when Jesus calls to the greedy, low-life tax collector perched on a limb. Worse, Jesus invites himself over to Zaccheus' house. Some grumble over Jesus' generosity and willingness to associate with the unclean. Yet when Zaccheus—a man who has been forbidden to enter the temple—meets Jesus, he repents and radically changes his life, promising to pay back in abundance everyone he has defrauded.

Jesus declares that salvation has come to Zaccheus' house; he too is a son of Abraham. Then Jesus proclaims that he has come to "seek and save" that which is lost. The listening crowd would have recognized the twofold reference to the prophecy of Ezekiel 34: Destruction was certain for bad shepherds, and God, as the Good Shepherd, was going to seek and find his lost sheep.

Explaining how the two kinds of shepherds are sharply contrasted throughout Scripture, I asked Lynne if she had ever known a bad shepherd.

"It's even hard for me to say the words 'bad shepherd,'" said Lynne, "because if you're a bad shepherd you're really a nonshepherd. I've seen people who own or manage sheep and are abusive toward them. Sometimes they're brutal. I sold several Shetlands to a family who allowed the young ewes to get pregnant with big Romneys—sheep that were three times their size. Because of the size difference, the ewes couldn't carry the fetuses, and the offspring died in the womb or at birth. Sometimes the ewes died too, because of the impossible labor.

"A lot of people don't pay attention to their sheep," Lynne continued. "I'll have people tell me they want to buy a sheep to cut their grass.

I'll ask if the person has a barn, and they'll say they have a tree. That's not a bad shepherd—that's a nonshepherd."

I pressed Lynne for some specific examples of bad shepherding. She recalled a couple who kept sheep for the tax benefits. They didn't like the animals, and when the lambing season arrived, they went on vacation and left the flock with a caretaker who didn't know anything about sheep. A friend of Lynne's received a phone call from the man who said something was hanging out of one of the sheep's backsides.

When Lynne's friend arrived, she found a dead lamb, only half-delivered. Several other lambs drowned in mud puddles after birth because no one was there to care for them.

My muscles tensed as Lynne described the neglect. I winced at the graphic portrait of a bad shepherd. Lynne's emotions awakened a sense of injustice inside of me; they also stirred my gratitude for good shepherds. I was thankful I had the opportunity to see Lynne interact with her sheep.

I had many other Scriptures I wanted to explore with Lynne, but our time together was coming to a close. I couldn't resist asking a final, more personal, question.

"Do you ever see characteristics of God revealed in your interaction with sheep?"

After a pause, Lynne responded, "I see compassion. Generally, even if a sheep is aggressive or a total brat, you still provide and care for it. You don't give up. You persist. You accept the differences between the sheep. And I find a great respect for life. These creatures have life, and I have the privilege of sustaining and nurturing it. That makes compassion come alive inside of me."

"And your favorite qualities of your favorite sheep?" I asked, my inquisitive nature getting the best of me.

"They come when I call their names," Lynne said. "They love me. They paw me and want my attention. They are responsive to me. They are not too afraid or flighty."

Before I could press my fingers against my lips, a huge yawn escaped.

"Tired?"

"No, I'm . . ." My mind searched for the right words to describe the unfamiliar sensation.

"I'm relaxed."

Lynne smiled wider than I'd seen in all our time together. The rhythm of her rocking chair made her look like she was nodding at me. Maybe she was.

"I see the Scripture differently thanks to my time with you," I said.

"Me too," Lynne said. "In fact, I never knew there were so many Scriptures that had to do with sheep. Will you send me what you've collected?"

I promised her I would.

Leif and Tom made their way into the living room with triumphant expressions. They announced that they had successfully wired several light fixtures in the new room in the barn. Lynne's renovated space was one step closer to being ready for her watchful eye around the clock during birthing season.

It was past time to go and Leif had already loaded our bags into the rental car, but I didn't want to leave. This place, this space, had become a respite I hadn't known I needed.

I wanted to see the sheep one last time. Lynne and I walked back to the barn, and I said my goodbyes. I visited Piaget's pen and looked at her gentle, endearing face and head tilt. I offered up a quiet prayer, asking God to spare this creature's life.

Lynne hugged me before I slipped into the passenger seat of the rental car. Then she tapped on the window and held up her index finger. She disappeared back into the barn and emerged a few moments later with treasures of the farm in her hands: peacock feathers and a quart-size Ziploc bag of wool from several of her sheep—including Piaget.

1.16 | Homeward Bound

I returned home exhausted and grateful. Opening one of the bags of wool Lynne gave me, I rubbed my fingers against the white downy softness. As I brought the wool close to my face to feel the texture, I inhaled the sharp skunky odor and coughed from the potency. When I was with the sheep, I never noticed their odor—in fact, what I did smell was almost pleasant, like damp green grass. I didn't realize that over the course of the weekend I started smelling like sheep—my clothes, my hair, everything. That's the nature of spending time as a shepherd: you smell like those you serve and protect.

My clothes went straight from the suitcase to the washing machine, but I was less sure of what to do with the thick layer of muck and feces that caked my boots. I soaked the soles in an inch of water in the garage overnight to no avail. Finally, I found a screwdriver in a toolbox and began chiseling off the earthy mixture that clung like dry cement.

Taking care of sheep has a way of sticking with you.

As I continued to dig between the treads of my shoes, I realized that my weekend with the shepherd did more than open my eyes to passages of Scripture; it opened my heart anew to God.

Sitting in front of the crackling fire, I flashed back to the moment I asked Lynne to read the entire chapter of John 10 aloud. As she got to the middle portion, she paused after each phrase, weighing it in her mind.

> "I am the good shepherd . . . the good shepherd lays down His life for the sheep . . . He who is a hired hand, and not a shepherd, who is not the owner of the sheep . . . sees the wolf coming . . . and leaves the sheep and flees . . . and the wolf snatches them and scatters them . . . He flees because he is a hired hand . . . and is not concerned about the sheep. I am the good shepherd . . . and I know My own and My own know Me . . . even as the Father knows Me . . . and I know the Father . . . and I lay down My life for the sheep" (John 10:11–15).

When I asked Lynne what she thought of the passage, her response was jarringly straightforward, "It's all true." So true that she had little comment to offer. She read the Scripture almost like a checklist.

> He who enters by the door is indeed the shepherd. Check.
> He calls his sheep by name. Check.
> He leads them out. Check.
> He goes before them and the sheep follow. Check.
> If a stranger comes and opens my gate, the sheep would run
>   away from him. Check.

Described as the "Shepherd of Israel," God promises never to leave nor forsake his flock. He guards confidently, watches keenly, and searches diligently. This was the mission of Jesus.

Jesus describes himself as the Good Shepherd, but I never knew what that meant until I spent time with sheep. Born in a stable, Jesus entered the straw and mud-poo of our world for one reason: Love. Love alone is what makes a shepherd good.

If Lynne spent so much time caring and being concerned for her sheep, how much more does God care and demonstrate his concern for each of us?

Like the story Lynne told me of one of her young rams, we all are tempted to stick our necks out through the fence to nibble on what looks like sweeter grass. When we find our horns caught and we're in trouble, only the Good Shepherd can set us free, and he does it time and time again.

Though I memorized Psalm 23 as a child, rereading the passage brought new comfort to my soul. *The Lord is my shepherd, and I shall not want. He is enough. Period.*

Though this Psalm often garners the most attention as a shepherding passage, one of the most beautiful portraits of God as shepherd is tucked away in Isaiah 40:11:

> Like a shepherd He will tend His flock,
> In His arm He will gather the lambs
> And carry them in His bosom;
> He will gently lead the nursing ewes.

The one described as "the great Shepherd of the sheep," the "Shepherd and Guardian of your souls," and "the Chief Shepherd" is the one whose lead I am called to follow. Some days he will lead me beside still waters. Other days he will lead me to lush fields.

And still others, he will lead me on the narrow, muddy path that connects them. Through it all, God is always the Good Shepherd.

Success! My left shoe was finally clean. As I stretched my fingers before starting the next maze of caked tread, I realized that one of the most meaningful spiritual lessons about God as the shepherd came from the geese in the barn. I remembered that they were constantly walking around.

"What are they looking for?" I asked Lynne.

"They're looking for their eggs," she said.

"Where are they?" I asked.

"I threw them in the creek," she said.

My eyes bugged in disbelief. I couldn't help blurting out, "Why?" Lynne's action seemed cold and cruel—a far cry from the woman who loved her sheep.

"Because they were infertile," she said. "They will never hatch. I need to get these geese back to their regular life. For three months they've been sitting on infertile eggs. The only way to get them back to the way they're supposed to be living is to take away their dead eggs."

Her answer helped me understand her action as one of compassion and wisdom. I couldn't help but wonder how often I have sat on dreams that were never going to come to fruition or, worse, sat on the empty promises of the enemy that would never yield life—only self-destruction and death.

As I thought back to the numerous times where God has been faithful to remind me, "It's time to get back to the life I've given

you," I recognized that this painful lesson isn't something I learn only once and move on. Like much of the spiritual insight I found on my trip to visit a shepherd, I will need to process, apply, refine, and reapply again and again the truth of what it means to live under the guidance of the Good Shepherd. Every step of the way, I'll strive to trust God.

With both shoes finally clean, I thought of Lynne and imagined Mario and Miguel resting in her arms as they sat at the crest of the high pasture, content to know that the needs of that moment were met by a good and faithful shepherd. So we too will rest in the arms of the good and faithful Shepherd who is the same yesterday, today, and forever.

PART II 🌾 The Harvest

2.1 | Everyone Needs a Joe

Leif and I met Joe in Juneau, Alaska, when he and a group of his college-aged friends wandered into our church. In an instant, we pegged them as out-of-towners.

"They're not from around here," Leif whispered. "Can we have them over?"

With the final words of the benediction, we rushed over to the young men and asked if they were visiting Juneau. Bewildered, one of them asked, "How'd you know?"

"The umbrellas gave you away," Leif said. "None of the locals use them."

We learned that this six-pack of guys was part of a larger team of faith-filled college students who had traveled to Juneau for the summer to serve the community and grow spiritually. We let them know that our house was open if they wanted home-cooked meals on Sunday afternoons. When you're a college student, the only thing better than food is free food, so we weren't surprised when they jumped at the opportunity.

Throughout the summer we saw the guys many times—now sans umbrellas—attending church, hanging out downtown, and crowding around our dining room table enjoying second and third helpings. We always tried to include a few vegetables in every meal after one of them mentioned the only green food he'd eaten in the last two months was in a box of Fruit Loops. After lunch most of the students disappeared, except for one who never seemed in a hurry to go anywhere: Joe.

With sandy-brown curlicue hair and a big smile, this Nebraska native became a regular at our house. Sprawling on our oversized chair, he talked with us about anything and everything. Lunch leftovers became dinner. Our conversations orbited around life, God, and relationships, with too many pee-your-pants bouts of laughter to count.

During late-night conversations, we got to know Joe's story. His dad had left when he was only three. Surviving on welfare and food stamps, Joe's mom, a woman of deep courage and faith, worked at an egg factory during the day and took classes at night until she earned a nursing degree. She made sure her three sons knew two things: they were loved, and God was the source of everything.

Joe's uncle Aaron became a father figure to him. With a twinkle in his eye, Joe recalled the times that his mom let him skip school on his birthday to help repair fences on his uncle's farm.

"That's when I fell in love with farming," Joe said. "My uncle let me ride around in the tractor during harvest. That was my favorite season of all—at the end of it you can climb into the granary and jump in the harvest you just brought in!"

The picture of Joe leaping into a silver silo brimming with golden corn brought a smile to my face.

Throughout the summer, Joe entertained us with his homegrown farming stories and random insights on life. One unforgettable day, Joe taught us about the "wenis." He kept grabbing our elbows and saying, "I've got your wenis." Since the word sounded terribly inappropriate, I asked Joe to explain.

"My mom is a nurse, and she taught us that the loose skin around your elbow is called a wenis," Joe said.

"That's ridiculous! There's no way it's called a wenis," I protested.

Joe went to the source of all such nonsense—urbandictionary .com—to prove his point. He was right. To this day, Leif and I will occasionally grab each other's elbows and giggle in honor of Joe.

At the end of the summer, Joe returned to Wayne State in Nebraska for his junior year. We thought that would be the last we'd hear from him. Fortunately, we were wrong.

Joe continued to call us every few weeks once he was back in Nebraska. He gave us the lowdown on his latest girlfriend, part-time job, and family. We shared our latest news and exchanged areas where prayer was needed. Those calls began almost five years ago, and they continue today.

2.2 | Seasons of Friendship

After I spent time with Lynne, I wanted to dig more into the agrarian themes of Scripture. With so many references to fields and harvest planted throughout the Old and New Testaments, I became convinced that a farmer would have rich insights. When I mentioned the idea to Leif, he suggested that I call Joe.

I dismissed the idea. "Joe's not a full-time farmer."

"But he grew up farming, and his uncle's a farmer," Leif argued. "You could sit down with them together."

At the first hint that we might visit, Joe yelled with glee, "You're coming to Nebraska!"

I'm still not sure Joe really heard my reason for wanting to get down in the Nebraska dirt—that I wanted to find the connection with God and the Scriptures—but Joe assured me that he and his uncle were happy to spend time talking about farming. Our trip was scheduled during the first alfalfa harvest. We flew into Omaha, drove to Sioux City, and Joe met us after we checked into our hotel.

Dressed in shorts, a T-shirt, blue flip-flops, and his signature backward ball cap, Joe greeted us with his trademark smile. Wrapping his thick arms around us, he gave us bear hugs—attempting to lift both of us off the ground. While he whirled me around in the air with ease, Leif was a bigger challenge. Ever determined, Joe managed to hoist my six-foot-eight Alaskan two whole inches off the floor.

We enjoyed our evening of laughter and reminiscing. At one point, I asked Joe why he spent so much time at our house when he was in Alaska. "It was the chair," Joe said. "Your chair rocked. Do you still have it?"

With a straight face, I leaned toward Joe. "I'm sorry to have to tell you this, Joe," I deadpanned, "but—this is harder to say than I thought it would be—we sold it when we left Alaska."

As our laughter died down, Joe grew serious. "I came over because I had just gotten out of a relationship, and it was really hard," Joe recalled. "Your house was like a sanctuary. Leif and I had really good talks, and I enjoyed the friendship. Plus, you had good food and a sweet chair."

Note to self: Always invest in a comfy chair.

Talking late into the evening, Joe reminded us of our adventures together that summer—painting the garage, experimenting with a Mountain Dew bread recipe—and, of course, the wenis.

"Tomorrow you're going to get to drive Big John," Joe promised.

"I've always wanted to drive a tractor," I said. "*Vroom. Vroom.*"

"That's not exactly what a tractor sounds like," Joe corrected.

"Barroom-broom-broom-broom," I grunted.

"Now that's more like it," Joe said.

2.3 | Storing

The verdant hills that lined the half-hour drive to Aaron's farm mesmerized me. I couldn't help but notice something rhythmic about the hundreds of acres of corn, beans, and alfalfa we passed—each neat row zipping by at sixty-five miles per hour like the flickering images from an old silent movie.

As we drove back roads deeper into the farmland, Joe waved at many of the fellow drivers. He pointed to particular fields, naming the farmers and explaining how they knew his uncle.

"Among farmers around here, there's a real camaraderie and respect," Joe said. "Everyone knows each other. My uncle Aaron can drive down the road and point to almost every truck and tell you who owns it and how their crop is doing this year. 'Round here, people will leave their trucks in the field overnight, windows down, keys in the ignition."

Joe pointed to an open metal barn with five silver silos on the side of the road. He instructed us to pull over. "We're here!" he exclaimed with a grin.

Stepping out of the car, I knew I had arrived . . . in the middle of nowhere. Besides the barn, silos, two colorful stock cars, a Hot Slots billboard, and a few pieces of rusty equipment, rows of corn filled the landscape in every direction. I took in a deep breath and enjoyed the sweet musty fragrance of the fields.

As Joe began giving us a tour of the farm, a tongue of wind lapped a patch of dust, creating a tiny upward whirl. As we walked, Joe explained the purpose of each piece of equipment in the warehouse-sized barn, then took us around the back to look at the silos. He pointed to one whose roof and walls were mangled like a soda can in a recycling bin.

"That's what tornado-force winds can do," he said.

I suddenly realized how much more aware of the weather Joe, his uncles, and other farmers are—simply because of what they do. The power that caused that metal carnage sparked a rush of emotion, as I felt both angered and awed by the destruction and loss.

Walking toward one of the silos that was still intact, Joe asked if I wanted to see the corn inside. Eyeing the steep, narrow metal ladder on the side of the silo, I taunted, "You first!"

Joe scurried up the ladder in his flip-flops, flung open a metal door, and yelled down, "Empty."

I felt relieved. Realizing that I had only narrowly escaped swimming in a silo, I asked Joe if we could look inside the empty granary. He clambered down and opened a lower door. We peeked inside—only a handful of dried corn stippled the dusty floor. The faint scent of stale breakfast cereal filled my nose.

As we continued the tour, I couldn't help but think about a farming parable Jesus told. Encouraging his followers to be on their guard against all forms of greed, he described a rich farmer whose crop was so abundant that he didn't have any place to store it. Rather than give away or sell the excess, he decided to tear down his barns and build larger ones where he could store all his grain and goods. His reasoning was simple: With all his savings he could live a posh life, eating, drinking, and celebrating.

God called the rich farmer a fool. That night would be his last. All his abundance would go to someone else. The parable is not antiwealth, but rather centers on how to handle those seasons of life when wealth flows. The rich farmer didn't acquire his harvest through trickery or deceit; he simply had a great year.

In a prudent agricultural move, he builds vast storehouses to contain the excess. Yet God's issue is not with the size of his harvest or storage containers; it's with his heart. The farmer views the abundance as his own, and the greedy attitude is laid bare when he uses the word "I" six times to describe his accomplishment and plans for the future—without thought of God or others. The unmistakable mention of "my crops," "my barn," "my goods," and "my soul" eliminates the space for others or acknowledgment of God. This is the ultimate you-can't-take-it-with-you parable, or what I like to call the there-ain't-no-luggage-racks-on-the-hearse reminder.

2.4 | Sowing

"Are you ready to drive Big John?" Joe's voice broke through my brief reverie.

"Show me the tractor!"

We rounded the corner of the barn, and there sat Big John in all of his green glory. This was no ordinary tractor. This was a John Deere 8430. In the farming community, those numbers meant it had racing stripes. Since its tires were as tall as I was, I felt grateful for the steps and scrambled inside. Joe and I scrunched together on the seat as he explained all the gears.

"You just turn the ignition, push in the clutch, and pull back on the red handle," he instructed. I was ready to put the plan and Big John into motion except for one glitch: my legs were too short to reach the clutch and foot pedals.

"I'll help you," Joe offered. I scooted over in the seat and Joe pressed down on the clutch. Big John roared to life. I bumped the red handle for speed. Big John sputtered. As we edged forward, I felt exhilaration mixed with sheer terror. I had never driven anything so ginormous in my life. If we crashed, I'd get a real good sense for how a farmer understood the Bible since I'd be working off my debt to Uncle Aaron forever.

As we maneuvered around the farm, I asked Joe about a device on the dashboard. Joe explained that the machine helped his uncle control the seed population during the planting season. A good farmer knows his land so well that when he comes to an area that has more sand than soil, he'll decrease the number of seeds that are released, knowing the land is less productive.

"Sounds like the parable of the sower," I said.

"I think about that a lot," Joe agreed. "If my uncle Aaron knows his land so well that he can tell just the right amount of seeds to release at just the right time of year to bring a fruitful harvest, how much more does God know you and me?"

I was intrigued by Joe's remark. In Jesus' story, a farmer plants seeds by hand (no John Deere for this guy). As he goes, some of the seeds are eaten by birds. Others land on thin soil and though the seeds sprout, the soil lacks depth, causing the tender plants to die in the heat of the day. Other seeds fall among thorns, which rob them of the nutrients they need to survive. Still others are sprinkled on good ground. Not only do these healthy seeds sprout and survive, but they thrive, producing an exponentially fruitful crop.

"If Aaron knows some of his land has sand and rocks, why does he still plant there?" I asked.

"Uncle Aaron knows that even those areas may produce some fruit. They will never produce as much—which is why he doesn't invest as much seed in those areas. Instead, he focuses on the best ground to work with."

I was taken by Joe's observation that the sandy and rocky areas of the land were still productive on some level. All too often I look at those rugged areas in my own life and think nothing good can come from them. I want to dismiss them altogether, but the image of Aaron still choosing to plant—albeit not as many seeds—challenged my notion. While the stony areas in my life may not compare in outward productivity, there is no area of my life that is above (or below) the potential for redemption, restoration, or use by God.

One place in my life where I've been seeing God's growth—despite the hardness of my heart—is the area of faith. Recently, a low-income church that we support discovered that they had to leave the building they were leasing because it was being sold. They felt like they were supposed to buy a small building nearby, but in their urban environment they struggled to find a place that would meet their needs for less than a million dollars. Miraculously, they found one that was being sold at auction, but the cost of the

building was still more than six times the church's annual budget, and their requests for a bank loan were denied. They had thirty days to raise the full amount for the building. I thought it was impossible and didn't financially support the effort. But within thirty days, the congregation secured more than two-thirds of the money needed and a bridge loan from Christian businessmen to cover the additional costs. Today, the church meets in that building—paid in full.

I was grateful and humbled to see God work through followers of Jesus from around the country to do what I considered impossible. For this tiny community to raise so much money so quickly was what I consider miraculous. The event unveiled the stoniness of my own heart. As I prayed, I felt like the Lord firmly corrected me, "You have no idea what I'm capable of!"

I still think about that sacred echo, and the reality that God is still working in this area of my life. Though my faith may be weak—at times, nonexistent—God is still preparing the soil of my heart for greater things.

As we rounded the farm for a final lap, I felt a gust of wind burst through an open window. The earthy scent of the land filled my nostrils.

"Sometimes when you read something in the Bible, it's got some big religious meaning," Joe said. "But when you live in the environment that's described in the Bible, it comes to life in a whole new way. You begin to realize that God isn't just saying something as an analogy; he's really saying it. So when God created the world, he had it in mind to use all these things as examples to teach us."

Feeling more comfortable and courageous behind the wheel, I bumped the throttle forward with the fleshy part of my palm. Big John coughed with excitement and picked up speed.

"What's a specific spiritual lesson you've learned from growing up around farming?" I asked.

"Do you know how the Bible talks about firstfruits?"

I nodded, remembering the instruction God gave to the Israelites that they were to take the firstfruits of their produce to the priest in a basket as an offering. The firstfruits in the New Testament represent the first part of a blessing, the promise that there's more to come.

"Well, it's different for us than in ancient times, because we don't take our produce as an offering to the priest," Joe said. "But every season, my family still enjoys the firstfruits of the harvest. One of the things our family does is get together as soon as the corn and tomatoes and other vegetables and fruits are ripe. We spend an entire day picking, cleaning, and canning. Grandpa will bring some of the watermelons he's grown. He'll break them over his leg and give us each huge chunks. We'll eat until we can't eat another bite and wipe our sticky hands on our pants. Then we'll share with friends, extended family members, and those we know who are in need. I love those days."

"So for you, firstfruits isn't just a concept?" I clarified.

"It's part of how we live," Joe said.

Looking across the expansive fields, I knew I didn't have a clue of the hard work and countless demands that lined every day, but I was grateful for the opportunity to experience a taste of the farming world—if only for a short time.

"How do I stop?" I asked, rounding the corner toward the homestretch.

"Asking questions?" Joe replied.

"No—the tractor."

Since my toes couldn't reach the brake, Joe stomped on the pedal for me and volunteered to park Big John. I climbed out of the tractor and ran toward Leif.

"What did you think?" Leif asked.

"I want one!" I said. "Could we build a bigger garage?"

2.5 | It All Comes Out in the Field

We spent the rest of the afternoon exploring the farm. The machinery reminded me that farming had come a long way over the last few thousand years. Plowing and sowing used to be one operation, with grain scattered from an open basket tied onto the back of a donkey. The Babylonians invented a primitive seed drill that would penetrate the soil so the seeds weren't stolen by the birds.

Without access to a Big John (or a little one!), many farmers in biblical times used plows attached to a yoke that went over the necks of animals who did the work of preparing the soil. Oxen were the animals of choice. Biblical law forbade the mixing of two different animals, such as a donkey and an ox, because the unequal pull would cause the weaker animal to suffer.

In the early evening, we decided to grab dinner together. On the way to a local restaurant named Bob's that served the biggest portion of fries I'd ever seen, I once again found myself mesmerized by the well-organized queues of corn in the fields we passed. While the rows of most farms were aligned and looked like works of art, a few were overgrown with weeds and didn't look as well cared for around the edges.

"Why do some fields look so different?" I asked Joe.

"As farmers, we tend to size each other up by how our fields look," Joe said. "If a farmer has crooked rows, he'll usually try to blame the new guy—someone who's a first-time hired hand. When you see a field that's planted straight and bulging with a healthy crop, you know the farmer has taken his time. But if you see a crop that's crooked or brown, you start to wonder why the farmer didn't spray, take better care of the crop, and invest more time in his fields."

"So it all comes out in the fields," I said.

"What do you mean?" Joe asked.

"I mean your fields reveal who you are as a farmer," I said. "Everyone has bad years, pests, and crazy stuff that happens, but if you watch over the long haul, year after year, then you can tell who's a good farmer and who's not."

"Exactly," Joe agreed.

The principle reminded me of Matthew 7:16, where Jesus says, "You will know them by their fruits." Just as grapes don't grow on thornbushes and figs don't spring out of thistles, a harmful weed cannot produce healthy fruit. Both vines and trees produce fruit that is consistent with their nature. Jesus offers this particular insight only a few moments after he's instructed his followers to avoid judging each other, suggesting that there's a balance between never judging and naively accepting everything.

This idea of examining the fruit reappears throughout the New Testament. It was John the Baptist who challenged the Pharisees and Sadducees to "bear fruit in keeping with repentance" (Matthew 3:8) and Paul who instructed the church of Galatia that those who are true followers will bear fruit of the Spirit rather than works of the flesh.

By the time we finished dinner, the sun was just beginning to dip below the horizon, casting a mosaic of shadows. As dusk relented to night, Joe reminded us that it wasn't too late to visit Uncle Aaron's.

2.6 | Disconnected

Preparing for my visit with Joe and Aaron, I found more than one hundred Scripture passages that describe the process of reaping and harvesting, but that was only the edge of my field of discovery. The Bible contains nearly three dozen references to plowing and three hundred references to fields. I was struck once again by the agrarian world that dominates the Bible from Genesis through the Gospels. It isn't until the adventures of Paul and the early church that we find the Scriptures speaking into and out of a more urban context.

Scripture tells us that God creates the heavens and the earth. Light separates from darkness. Sky separates from water. On the third day, land and sea separate. The first dry ground appears and promptly produces vegetation. In what's described as a single day, God forms soil, water sources, and reproductive plant life.

The following day brings order and time through the creation of the sun, moon, and corresponding seasons. On the fifth day, the ocean overflows with living creatures beyond imagination. The sixth day sees the earth filled with animals, and, finally, God creates Adam and Eve to rule over the earth and all its creatures. In Hebrew, *Adam* comes from *adamah*, which means ground or earth. It's a pun demonstrating the interplay between the first human being and the earth that sustains us and from which we come.

Filled with literary beauty, the creation story circles themes of time, weather, and agriculture throughout which God is the primary actor, artist, and designer. In Genesis 2, we learn that God formed human life "of dust from the ground," demonstrating the deep connection between the earth and ourselves. Adam and Eve's initial assignment from God is to care for or "keep" that which springs out of the ground—the garden. The word for keep (*shamar*) can be translated "guard," "take care of," or "look after" and indicates a loving, caring, and sustaining kind of keeping—not just of the land that produces food, but of all the land, reminding us of our environmental responsibility. This is the same root of the verb *shomer*, which is used in Psalm 121:4, describing God's careful watching over the psalmist. God promises he will neither slumber nor sleep as he cares for us.

After a tragic moment of willful disobedience, the assignment became exponentially more difficult. Cultivating the land required sweat, pain, and hard work. Thorns, weeds, pestilence, disease, and drought—all unknown before sin—entered everyday life in the fields. Eden, the paradise we've longed for ever since, was gone. Yet God continued—and continues—to call his children to care for and be connected to the earth. Even today, apart from healthy soil and water, life withers and dies.

Scripture is rooted deeply in agricultural themes. In order to "guard" and "take care of" the land, farmers had to know their land intimately, discovering how slight shifts in the weather, soil, and temperature affected a potential crop. With most of the information passed down from family members or those in a tight-knit Jewish community, the inter-connectedness between the people and land often ensured their ability to survive. Interestingly, it's the fifth commandment that connects honoring one's parents with the promise "that your days may be prolonged and that it may go well with you on the land (*adamah*) which the LORD your God gives you" (Deuteronomy 5:16).

Yet despite this unmistakable link between the people and the

land, I look under my fingernails and don't see any dirt. I'm disconnected from the agricultural world. Except for some plants my husband, Leif, nurtures in our home, and a few phone calls to ensure the college kid down the block really does mow our lawn, I don't have any sort of immediate connection to the land, and the more I read the Scriptures, the more I'm becoming convinced that maybe there's a better way.

2.7 | Digging in Scripture

As I scouted various Scriptures during early mornings of study, I discovered a link between the land and people's relationship with God. In the Old Testament, harvest represents abundance, the reward for labor, and a testimony of God's goodness and blessing. When Isaac sows seed on his land, he reaps a hundredfold in his harvest. Scripture is quick to note that the Lord blesses him. The shepherd-king, David, calls on God for abundance and blessing in the harvest. He petitions God that the barns would be full with every kind of produce.

Meanwhile, images of failed harvests are used by many of the prophets to represent God's judgment or an unwillingness of the people to follow God's law. In ancient societies, the harvest is a matter of life and death. Rain, drought, fire, and enemies didn't just threaten a crop but also the people's very survival, thus making the topic of harvest fertile ground for teaching and instruction. God uses three years of famine to get David's attention so that he seeks the face of the Lord again, and Job's testing includes severe harvest losses. Yet despite the link between the condition of the land and human responsiveness to God, it would be unfair to interpret every natural disaster as a sign of God's judgment or every abundant crop as a sign of God's approval.

Harvest also demonstrates the natural rhythm of our world. After the flood, God promises that as long as the earth remains, humanity will experience seedtime and harvest, cold and heat, summer and winter, day and night. In the book of Ecclesiastes, one of the darker philosophers of the Bible reminisces on such patterns and the promise that for everything there is a season. (Sorry, but you might be humming "Turn, Turn, Turn" for the rest of the day.)

The life and celebrations of the Jewish people often centered on harvests. Throughout the Scriptures, time is identified by a particular harvest. One of the encounters between sisters Leah and Rachel is noted as "in the days of wheat harvest" (Genesis 30:14), while Ruth and Naomi arrived in Bethlehem "at the beginning of barley harvest" (Ruth 1:22). While these unassuming mentions are easy to miss in casual reading, they point to the life of a people steeped in agrarian necessities.

Three significant festivals were based on the agrarian calendar. Passover coincided with the barley harvest, the Feast of Pentecost (also known as the Feast of Weeks) celebrated the wheat harvest, and the Feast of Booths aligned with the fruit harvest. In addition, the Feast of Firstfruits was based on an agricultural practice of farmers bringing a portion of their first produce to the priests. To this day, the book of Ruth—a story about redemption, as well as seasons and harvest—is often read during the Feast of Pentecost. A law from the Levitical code, which forbade farmers from harvesting the edges of the field, ensured that the poor and those in need could glean enough to live. This provision helped sustain Ruth and open the door to a new life.

As Jesus walked through fields with his disciples, the master storyteller used metaphors and images of planting and harvesting to teach spiritual lessons. He spoke of the crisis created by a shortage of workers during harvest time, the importance of planting in good soil, and the danger of trusting in bigger barns for provision—all themes those living in an agrarian society grasped.

Even a portrait from Revelation is the image of an angel reaping the harvest with a sharp sickle.

Throughout the Scriptures, God used harvest to teach the people principles of generosity, faithfulness, and restoration.

2.8 | Contentment

My mind brimmed with questions and ideas for Aaron. I couldn't wait to meet the man who had played such an important role in Joe's life. Pulling into the driveway, I noticed all the farming equipment and supplies that lined the property. Closer to the house, bikes and toys littered the lawn.

Joe was energized. "I can't wait to see my cousins!"

We let ourselves in through the gate of the white picket fence that bordered the front yard and were greeted by two dogs whose tails were wagging frantically. Aaron met us at the front door. He looked like a bigger version of Joe: straw-colored hair, deep blue eyes, and an engaging smile. His family welcomed us into a living room with toys and board games piled high against every wall.

"This is what happens when you try to raise four children and farm full-time," Aaron said.

"Actually, this happens to any family with four kids," I said with a smile.

We followed Aaron down the hallway into the kitchen; Joe hung out in the living room with the little ones. Grabbing a seat at the long wooden kitchen table, I began taking notes as Aaron spoke, his voice thick with a Midwestern twang. His tan told me he had spent long days in the fields, but the joy with which he talked about farming revealed his love for it. He began farming as a child on his father's land. They had a farm—only sixty acres—but used the produce to support and feed the family. Like Joe, Aaron eventually began working on his uncle's larger farm. A few years after graduating from high school, he began leasing his own acreage and focused on growing beans, corn, alfalfa, and wheat.

"It gets in your blood," Aaron said with confidence.

It also gets in your body, I thought, noting Aaron's burly frame and bear-paw-sized, calloused hands.

"What's sad is that even though my family was farm-oriented, I'm the only one left farming full-time. It's a sign that farming has gotten so tough—especially with the cost of land."

"Why do you do it then?" I asked, aware of the stress he must feel raising a family of four kids under such a fickle and demanding occupation.

"I do it for the love of it," Aaron said.

"Do you think farmers know or respect God more?" I asked.

"I can only speak for myself," Aaron said. "I have a lot of friends who were raised differently, but I know that when I plant a seed, without God nothing would come of it. I can do what I can do, but unless God blesses me I won't get a thing out of those fields."

2.9 | Chaff

Looking across the kitchen, I noticed a few sets of eyes watching with curiosity from the doorway. "If you get your jammies on, you can come in," Aaron said. "But just for a few more minutes."

One by one, the children filed around the kitchen table to listen

to our conversation, followed by Joe. Their young eyes grew wide when I pulled out my thick Bible.

"That's a big one!" one of the older children exclaimed.

"They make 'em a lot smaller these days," I replied. "Even your size."

Opening the thin pages, I decided to ask Aaron about a familiar story in Luke, the one of a man who sincerely wants to follow Jesus, but who asks to return home first to say goodbye to his family. Jesus' response seems out of character, almost harsh, when he says that no one who places his hand on the plow and looks back is fit for service in God's kingdom. Clearly, following Jesus is not a hobby or part-time job, but a full-time endeavor. Though Aaron used Big John rather than a plow, I asked what Jesus' answer meant to him.

"If they're using a plow, that means it's planting season," Aaron explained. "If I look backward while I'm driving Big John, then I'm going to weave, which means I'll get bends in my rows."

I had read that in biblical times, plows were light and portable but could only scratch the surface of the ground to a depth of three or four inches. A farmer couldn't afford to look back, because he needed all his energy and focus to push down and dig deep enough into the ground. He also had to keep a careful watch for rocks and stones that would break the plow.

The machines used to plow today are much different, but Aaron still knew the importance of not looking back.

"Why is it bad to get bends in your rows?" I asked.

"Bends in the rows lead to a lot of inefficiency," Aaron said. "It's not the best possible use of your limited space. You can lose a lot of valuable farmland quickly, and without proper spacing, plants will be forced to compete against each other for nutrients and sunlight. If you've got straight rows, then it's easy to keep them straight, but once you get a curve in a row, it's very hard to get the rows straight again. The only way to fix it is to look for a marker far in the distance and set your eyes straight ahead on that marker."

Aaron's words reminded me of how small compromises in my own life can lead to big consequences. I appreciated the idea of looking for something, or rather Someone, ahead in the distance to reset onto the right course. The concept of raising up a marker or a banner is found throughout Scripture, from the bronze snake raised in the wilderness that brings healing to Jesus' promise that when he is raised up he will draw all people to himself. Paul reminds us to keep our eyes fixed on Jesus, the author and perfecter of faith.

Recognizing that Aaron was connecting with ease to the agriculture metaphors of Jesus, I flipped open my Bible to another teaching, the story in Matthew 13 of the tares that were planted in a wheat field by an enemy of the farmer. The parable is one of the few that Jesus explains in detail to his followers. Unlike many of his other stories, Jesus identifies the characters in this parable. The one who sows the good seed is the Son of Man. The fields are the world. The good seeds are God's people, and the tares are planted by the evil one. At the end of the age, the Son of Man will send forth his angels, who will gather the tares and throw them into the fire, but the good seed—the righteous—will live forever.

"As a farmer, what does this mean to you?" I asked.

"I interpret the tares as wheat that doesn't have any seed," Aaron said. "If you're just walking through a field and looking at the wheat, then you can take for granted that all of it is good. But if you pluck a shaft of wheat and roll it in your fingers, you'll find that some shafts have good seed, while others have nothing at

all. They're empty husks. You can't tell in the fields, but it always shows up in the grain tank."

"So that's what John the Baptist was alluding to when he said that the coming Promised One would gather the wheat into the barn but burn up the tares?" I asked.

"Like Uncle Aaron said," Joe piped in, "you can't tell wheat from tares just by looking at it. You have to grab, squeeze, and crush it to find out whether it's real or not. I think that's true of the spiritual life. Some people can look really good on the outside—they can seem more mature or look like they really know their Bible—but when it comes to the pressures of life and getting crushed, that's when the fruit really shows."

My mind flashed to moments when I'd seen this principle demonstrated. I have known people who pursue everything in life with wild abandon except matters of the soul. They live waiting to be temporarily filled up by the next latest-and-greatest thing. I have known others who seemed concerned with spiritual matters on the outside, but when temptations or pressures of life exerted themselves, they deserted their faith. I have also seen those who, despite Job-like trials and temptations, hold on to God. Their goodness and faith shine like the noonday sun in the midst of the struggles they face.

Yet as Aaron spoke, the chaff I was most concerned about was not in someone else's life but in my own. Where were the hollow areas of my own heart? Where had I resisted the harvest God was trying to grow in me? Where was weakness and emptiness hiding within?

2.10 | Low Yields

Something kept bothering me about the concept of harvest. I thought of the Bible describing harvest as a time of gladness and a time when men enjoyed the fruits of the land. The setting for such gladness in Isaiah 9:3 is within the context of the promise of the birth of a child, Immanuel.

"What's it like being tossed to and fro between years of feast and famine?" I asked.

"A good harvest is euphoria," Aaron said. "It's when everything you've done culminates into a crop that is profitable and allows you to maintain your means and way of life."

I loved that image of extreme joy, but I knew not every year was an abundant year. How did Aaron and his family handle the bad years? As I looked around the kitchen, I could tell that this year had been abundant. An open pantry door revealed jars of colorful vegetables lining the shelves. The canned goods were too numerous to count. Signs of blessing were everywhere. How did the kitchen change in leaner years?

"A bad harvest is, well, an angry disappointment," Aaron said, his face dropping. "Once you do everything you can do, it's hard when it doesn't materialize or amount to anything. It feels like a punch in the gut."

"How do you handle it?" I wondered.

"In the difficult years, I don't blame God," Aaron said. "I take it as it is. It's either good or bad. I praise God for good yields, but I'm not angry with him for poor yields. I just don't go there."

"A lot of people do go there," I said, reflecting on the many people I know—including myself—who wrestle with disappointment and anger with God.

"It's part of the seasons," Aaron said. "You have good years and bad years. They can't all be good."

"But don't you still get mad?" I asked, pushing the issue.

"Blaming God for a bad harvest doesn't do anything to help prepare you for the next one," Aaron said. "If you spend your time and energy blaming God, then you probably won't take personal responsibility for some of your own mistakes during the planting or growing season. Blaming God won't make you a better farmer."

Or a better person, I thought. While blaming someone else is never productive, Aaron's matter-of-fact reply unearthed something else in me. I had noticed how people tend to fall into one of two camps when it comes to blessings: God either gets all the credit for the good, but never gets acknowledged for the bad, or God doesn't get a lick of credit for the good but gets blamed for all the bad. The apostle Paul seems to have discovered and demonstrated how to handle the extremes of need and nimiety when he describes what it means to be content in all circumstances.

The Bible is full of people expressing the full range of emotions with God. The Psalms give us a window into a healthy relationship with God, and it includes opening up all our feelings to him. In some particularly difficult times, King David even goes so far as to say that God seems like his enemy. The key is that all these emotions are expressed within the context of faith. David never doubts that God is there, but he may wonder why God has allowed certain things to happen (including a bad harvest). And this is okay. God never rebukes the psalmist for opening up to him. That's a good thing, because I find myself yo-yoing between emotional extremes more than I'd like to admit.

2.11 | The Farmer's Bond

With Joe, Aaron, and the rest of the family gathered around, I asked, "Do you mind if I ask you some specific questions about farming from the Bible?"

"Not at all."

I read to Aaron a passage from Proverbs that says he who gathers in summer is a son who acts wisely, but he who sleeps during harvest is a son who acts shamefully. In ancient times, the children reflected the family's honor or shame. The foolishness of the lazy son's behavior didn't just affect his reputation but that of his entire family—a reminder that our decisions have a communal effect.

"Do you know anyone who has slept through a harvest, so to speak?" I asked.

Aaron explained that back in the 1980s there were a lot of farmers who, because of the drops in commodity prices, were slow to harvest their crops. "They were unmotivated," Aaron said. "I saw guys who didn't get out there and get it done when they were supposed to. There were farmers who were still picking and harvesting their crops after the first snow. Those guys didn't make it. Most of them lost their farms."

"So there's no sleeping during harvest?" I confirmed.

Aaron laughed. "No sleeping allowed," he said. "Though it is bedtime for you kids."

With a few protests of "Aw, Dad!" the children disappeared to their rooms. Joe followed behind them promising to read one, *just one*, story. I knew he'd read two.

"Though everyone's working during harvest, Joe says there's also a camaraderie among the farmers," I said.

Aaron explained that while laziness has no place during harvest, he has seen farmers give up time in their own fields to help a

farmer in need. A few years ago, a longtime member of the farming community had a heart attack at the height of the harvest.

"Everyone took a break from their own fields, gathered together, and cleaned up his fields in no time at all," Aaron said. "No one charged him for gas or anything. Whether or not you're family, we all grew up together, so there's a bond."

I imagined a similar bond must have existed long ago. In extreme cases, ancient farmers had to walk for several hours to their fields. Since families often owned their own plots for growing wheat, barley, olives, figs, and vines, members of the family were dependent on those who worked the land for their survival. During planting and harvest seasons, many farmers built lean-tos in the field and lived in these from Sunday morning to Friday night, returning home to celebrate the Sabbath. I wondered if they too shared stories of pitching in when others were in need.

2.12 | Workers

Imagining how much work went into harvest, I reflected on the words of Jesus when he said that the harvest was plentiful, but the workers were few, and how he encouraged his followers to pray that the Lord of the harvest send out workers. The Lord of the harvest is God, and the workers are those who respond to the prayer. The fact that Jesus says the workers are few speaks not only about the original twelve who are sent on a specific mission, but also about the mission of workers throughout the ages who are called to serve.

"What about finding qualified workers for your own fields?" I asked.

"Even with technology, that's a huge issue," Aaron said.

He explained that when he graduated from high school, the average farm was six hundred acres. That's about twelve blocks by twelve blocks for us city dwellers. Today it's more than six thousand acres. The upside is that fewer workers can get the job done because of advancements in technology, but finding those workers is as difficult as ever.

"There isn't anything about farming that would be difficult for someone to learn," Aaron said. "The problem is that too few workers want to learn."

As Aaron spoke, I couldn't help but wonder about the shortage of workers—not just on the farm but in the church too. Much work still needs to be done in our communities and around the world. Whether it's preaching the good news of hope found in Jesus or living out the trinity of faith, hope, and love, we exist in a time when all hands are needed on deck. I can't help but feel the same sense of urgency about the shortage of workers that Aaron has when he looks out on his fields. If the harvest isn't gathered, it will rot in the fields.

Time is short. The need is great.

That thought brought me to a passage that dealt with the attitude of the workers. In Luke 17, Jesus contrasts two servants. The first returned from the fields and demanded his meal. The second came in from the fields and prepared dinner for his master before eating. Jesus instructs his followers, "When you do all the things which are commanded you, say, 'We are unworthy slaves; we have done only that which we ought to have done.'"

I read this story to Aaron and asked if he'd ever experienced anything like it as a farmer.

"It's hard to find people who want to put in a good day's work," he said. "There's just too many ways of getting out of work. If you

have a guy who wants to work, you'll know it right away. A guy who doesn't want to work, you'll know it right away too."

Even in the church, it's easy to recognize those who are quick to say "yes!" to the spotlight but turn away when faced with the responsibility and hard work that accompany the job. A few years ago I listened to a well-respected, prominent pastor describe those who regularly approached him saying they wanted to do exactly what he was doing. His response still echoes in my mind, "You want the title and the stage, but you don't want to have to pay the price."

One of Aaron's biggest struggles isn't just finding people who want to work, but those who know how to use modern machinery. With countless technological advancements in farming, new devices require finding skilled workers who know how to use them and aren't afraid of physical labor.

I realized what Aaron experienced at the farm and what most leaders experience in the church isn't too different. With the ever-changing new developments in technology, it can be a challenge to keep adapting to new strategies and best practices and find quality workers willing to do the job and learn to use the right tools. As servants of God, we must be ready to work and serve, not out of merit or ease or what makes us feel the best but out of faithfulness.

2.13 | The Great Wait

I had one other verse I wanted to ask Aaron about—the image described in Revelation 14 of the Son of Man holding a sharp sickle in his hand. An angel from the temple cries out, "Put in your sickle and reap, for the hour to reap has come, because the harvest of the earth is ripe" (Revelation 14:14–16). The image is an apocalyptic metaphor, and I wondered about Aaron's response as I read the passage aloud.

"When I hear that, I think about how you can't rush the maturing process of a plant," Aaron said. "Every day has its own amount of growing units. Now, weather can affect the process, but at the end of the day, I can't change the weather. When you read that passage, I know that day is coming, but I can't make it come faster or slower. I can only choose how I live today."

Amen, I thought. Aaron's words reminded me that when it comes to harvesting a field, everything grows in its proper season and cannot be forced or hurried on a whim. Yet despite that reality, all too often I find myself in a rush, even wanting to do things to hasten the end of days. Is that really my place?

Harvest does not happen apart from waiting. When I think about harvest in these terms, my own impatience becomes more apparent. I plant a seed hoping it sprouts as quickly and dramatically as in the story of Jack and the beanstalk. But that isn't realistic.

Awhile back, Leif came home with a plant-your-own blue spruce. It was only a cup of dirt with a few seeds, but I knew he had just come home with our Christmas tree. We planted the little guy and named him Charlie, but seven months later, with the holiday season in full swing, our baby tree was only an inch tall and not strong enough to hold any ornaments that were not made from cotton balls. We still have Charlie, and we're hopeful that one day he will stand tall and beautiful. Until then, we have to wait.

With Joe helping to put his cousins to bed, I had the opportunity to ask Aaron something I had wondered about for years. Many of my friends who were raised by their mothers weren't as fortunate as Joe to have a father figure.

"What made you do it?" I asked. "What made you get involved in Joe's life?"

"I knew something was missing in his life, and while I couldn't provide everything, I knew that I could pick him up from school and let him drive the tractor with me," Aaron said. "It didn't cost me nothing. Nope, it didn't cost me nothing at all."

As I listened to Aaron talk about his intentional relationship with Joe, I could see how planting seeds of love and care in the lives of others can bear much fruit. In a much smaller way, we had experienced the same thing with Joe. We opened the door of our lives to a college student from Nebraska and he never left. For that, we are grateful. But what if we were even more willing to include others in our everyday lives? What if we were willing to invest in people for the long haul, through thick and thin? How much more fruitful would we be? Even if the invitation was simply running errands or hanging out on a great couch, what kind of difference would it make? If Joe was any kind of example, then maybe such humble actions really could change the world.

"Thank you, Aaron," I said.

"For what?"

"For being you," I said. "And thanks for loving Joe."

"It ain't nothin'."

"You can claim it ain't nothin', but let me tell you, it's a big something."

Joe bounded back into the room after tucking his cousins into bed. Pushing my chair back from the kitchen table, I thanked Aaron for his generous time and insights. "Keep an eye on this guy," I said, punching Joe's shoulder with my knuckles.

"Will do," Aaron said, his eyes reflecting the seriousness of his promise.

As the screen door closed behind us, I stared into the darkness of night. I breathed in the damp smell of farmland and exhaled a deep sigh of contentment. The moon peeked through a patch of thick trees on an adjacent hill, and I smiled at a sky filled with more stars than I had seen in a long time.

2.14 | Canning Tomatoes

Joe came by the next morning so we could meet his mom for lunch at a local eatery. He drove us to a Chinese dive downtown, and when she walked in, I easily recognized the curly sandy hair, sturdy frame, and sapphire eyes—Joe's mother. Eleanor had just finished an overnight shift at the hospital. Though exhausted, she greeted us with a warm hug and thoughtful conversation. Over huge plates of kung pao chicken and Mongolian beef, we enjoyed listening to the easy banter between Joe and his mom. They were used to giving each other a hard time—but make no mistake, Joe's mom always won.

As we chatted, Eleanor mentioned that she was behind on canning her tomatoes because she had picked up extra shifts at the hospital.

"They're just going to rot on the vine if I don't get to them," she said.

"We could help you!" I offered. "Right, Joe?"

Joe gave me a steely-eyed, I'm-gonna-kill-you glance.

"Joe doesn't like canning tomatoes," Eleanor said.

"I've done it too many times," Joe said.

"But never with us," I protested.

When Joe didn't say anything, I tried a different tactic. "I bet Joe

would love to can tomatoes for the loving mom who has worked so hard to support him, nurture him, and care for him for all these years," I said with a twinkle in my eyes.

"Fine," Joe said.

"Wahoo! We're canning tomatoes in Nebraska!"

After lunch, we drove to the house where Joe grew up. Picking our way through a garage chockablock with old wood, dusty tools, and unmarked boxes, we were welcomed into a sparse dining room separated from the kitchen by a narrow counter. While Leif and Joe went out to pick the tomatoes from the backyard garden plot, I tried to help Eleanor set up the stations for canning—washing, drying, peeling, de-seeding, chopping, cooking, and finally putting them in the jars. We chatted until everything was prepped and the tomatoes were inside. We had to wait until the huge pot of water was boiling before we could begin the canning process, so I pulled my Bible out of my bag and asked Joe if I could ask him about some more Scriptures.

Joe pushed his feet out from the chair, crossed his arms and legs, and drawled, "I'm ready when you are!"

I was curious how Joe responded to the biblical Joseph's dream—and not just because they shared the same name. As a young boy, Joseph finds favor with his father, who is unable to hide his affection for this particular son. One night Joseph has a dream that he and his brothers are out in the field binding grain together when suddenly Joseph's sheaf stands upright and all the other sheaves gathered around bow down to it. When Joseph shares the dream with his brothers, they are furious.

"Now that's just dumb," Joe said. "Anyone who shares that kind of dream is going to make people mad. A farmer naturally takes pride in the product he has, but you don't have to rub it in other people's faces like that."

Joe explained that most farmers become loyal to particular brands of seed, fertilizer, and machinery because they believe they work the best. At the feed stores, they'll sit around and argue about whose seed didn't do as well that year.

"What Joseph did, you just don't do," Joe said. "It's like me walking into the local store and saying to another farmer, 'Hey, it looks like your corn blew over—no, wait, it's just bowing down to mine.' Those are definitely fighting words."

As the water reached a rolling boil on the stove, Eleanor popped into the conversation and announced, "We're ready!"

Pointing to different areas of the kitchen, she described her process of canning—from the washing of the tomatoes, to dipping them in boiling water until the skin cracked, to cooling, skinning, and removing spots and blemishes.

"If you and Leif and Joe can take care of those, I'll take care of the rest of the canning process," she said.

"I call skinning the tomatoes," I yelled like a teenager calling shotgun.

While Leif washed the tomatoes, Joe helped with the canning. "So Joe, can I keep asking you questions?" I asked.

"As long as you can 'ketchup,'" he said, tossing me a juicy tomato.

Without a dish towel in sight, I wiped my hands on my jeans and pulled a crumpled sheet of notes out of my bag. I laid it flat on the kitchen counter safely away from the spray of tomato juice.

2.15 | Gleaning Treasures

Another passage that intrigued me was the teaching about the Sabbath. One of the Ten Commandments states that work is permitted six days a week, but the seventh day is designed for rest—even during plowing and harvest time.

"It's like they went out of the way to say that this commandment applies to farmers too," I said.

"That doesn't surprise me," Joe said. "When it's harvest time, it's hard to take a day off to rest and relax; when you see good weather, your field is ready, and everything is good to go. You don't know what tomorrow is going to bring—including frost and the first snow. That extra day of waiting could mean you lose your crop."

Lynne had identified a similar dependence on God whenever the best sheep were sacrificed. Whether centered around livestock or crops, the commands of God kept echoing this issue of trust and faith in him.

"Am I doing this right?" I asked, holding up my first attempt—a juicy, skinless tomato.

"You'll want to nip those too," Eleanor said, pointing out a few white spots. "They get tough if you try to can them, and one bad tomato can ruin the whole batch."

Before reaching for another plump fruit, I read aloud a passage from my notes regarding the instruction in Leviticus that when you reap the harvest of the land, you're not supposed to reap the corners of the field or the leftovers known as gleanings, but leave them for the needy. The command closes, "I am the LORD your God" (Leviticus 23:22).

"What does this passage say about God? Us?" I asked, picking up speed with each tomato I touched.

Joe explained how his uncle once noticed some guys walking his fields after the harvest, picking up leftover ears of corn and tucking them into their oversized pockets.

"Uncle Aaron just let them have the corn," Joe said. "He figured they needed it to feed their chickens."

Joe was quick to point out that what those guys were doing was still work. In tending the field, it's not just the farmer who has to work hard, but the gleaners, too, as they gather the leftovers.

"What that says about God is that he has blessed us with so much," Joe said. "And we need to leave some for those who aren't as fortunate, so they can receive a blessing from God too. But the deeper issue here is a heart one."

"What do you mean?" I asked as I plopped a tomato into Joe's to-do bin.

"I think God wants us to understand that we don't need all that we think we do," Joe said. "Some years we'll set a goal for so many bushels but end up short after harvesting. The granary you saw won't be full. Sometimes, if we were to go glean and clean up the corners and scraps on every field, then we'd make up the difference. The principle of gleaning reminds us that even if we don't hit our goals, we'll still survive. Gleaning teaches us that it's not about having more, it's about having enough."

That seemed to be a lesson that had been echoing in my life. I shared with Joe a recent conversation with a close friend who ran a highly successful business. She was representing a client to another company and negotiating the contract.

In each section of the contract, she asked, "What's the most you've ever done?" Quite foolishly, the spokesperson of the company told her.

"Well, then we want ten percent more," she demanded.

The spokesperson never caught on to the simple negotiation tactic and conceded to every request for an increase.

"I won ten percent more on every point," my friend said. "But somehow I thought it would feel better than it did. My client didn't really need the money, and neither did I. What did I really win?"

Joe nodded thoughtfully.

"Gleaning teaches us we don't need it all," he said. "It gives us an opportunity to share a little bit of what God has given us with others. That's why gleaning is so good for the heart."

"How'd you get so smart?" I asked with a razzing tone.

"Watching Uncle Aaron," Joe said without hesitating. He explained how his uncle leases fields from retired farmers because he can't afford to buy the land. As part of the contract, he agrees to give the owners a percentage of the profits.

"Because all these retired farmers get a portion of the profits, they're invested in the land," Joe said. "If they're outside and see something that's not quite right, they'll call Uncle Aaron right away and let him know. In the same way, I bet that every so often a gleaner would tell a landowner if something wasn't quite right.

"When we think of others above ourselves, God has a way of blessing us," Joe continued. "It may not be monetarily, but he blesses our hearts, and that is a greater joy. Anyone willing to work can learn to raise a crop, but not just anyone can raise it in a way that helps others."

I felt a pair of eyes over my shoulder. Eleanor was assessing my work. "Do I get an A?" I asked.

"A-plus!" she exclaimed. "Anyone who can get Joe to help with canning gets an automatic A-plus in my book."

With some chores, time stands still, but with others the time seems to pass all too fast. As I handed the last tomato to Joe, I asked, "Is that it?"

"You're done," Eleanor affirmed.

I didn't want to be done. I wanted to stay.

Leif reminded me that we had a plane to catch.

"Let me count first!" I protested. In one afternoon, we had canned two dozen jars of fresh tomatoes. Eleanor was thrilled and so were we.

After a series of hugs, we said our goodbyes. Joe walked us out to the car and gave us each one last huge Alaskan bear hug. This time, he managed to lift Leif at least three inches off the ground.

2.16 | The Beauty of Harvest

As the airplane gained altitude, I watched with wonder as the buildings shrank and the land revealed acre after acre of crops in every direction. Farm country. From the sky, the fields looked like a patchwork quilt of squares and circles—their boundaries established by landowners and irrigation systems. Together, they offered a vibrant portrait of sowing, reaping, and the wait for harvest.

In my time with Joe, I felt like I had touched on the grittiness of the Bible—the dirt and soil that mark its pages from Genesis to Revelation. Even today, countless men and women are working in the fields. These servants are encouraging, loving, giving, and laying down their lives for something greater. In the process, we are moving toward a final harvest—that moment in time when evil is blown away like chaff and the redeemed are united with God.

When I heard the *ding* that reminded us it was now safe to turn on our portable electronic devices, I was still entranced by the landscape. I studied the fields, noting the ones that were more vibrant and those which had been neglected. What we sow, we will reap—maybe not today or tomorrow—but the day will come. When we plant good seed, the harvest is delicious, delectable. When we plant seed that's corrupt, the rotten fruit of our lives reveals it.

Neither Aaron nor Joe ever planted an acre of corn and expected the land to produce an acre of wheat. Yet how often in my own life am I surprised by the results of my own actions, even when they're not kind or righteous or just? How often do I have unrealistic expectations that I will reap where I never bothered to sow? I sometimes see this play out in my relationships. I'll expect that when I connect with an old friend, our time will be deep and meaningful. Instead, it ends up feeling shallow and forced because I haven't taken the time to steadily nurture the relationship. Unrealistic expectations also affect my spiritual life. I wonder why I feel distant from God, yet I haven't taken time to dig deeper into Scripture, pray, or serve others.

Galatians 6:7–8 instructs, "Do not be deceived, God is not mocked; for whatever a man sows, this he will also reap. For the one who sows to his own flesh will from the flesh reap corruption, but the one who sows to the Spirit will from the Spirit reap eternal life."

There's a lot at stake. If I could just get this one principle to take root in my heart, it would change the way I live—making me more intentional, more loving, and wiser in the words I use and actions I take. Though this scriptural principle induces a healthy amount of respect and fear, I believe it unleashes a much more powerful sense of hope. No wonder Paul concluded, "Let us not lose heart in doing good, for in due time we will reap if we do not grow weary" (Galatians 6:9).

When I embrace a life that is pleasing to God—one that chooses righteousness over being merely right, one that chooses kindness in the face of rejection, one that chooses love rather than silent withdrawal—something comes alive in my heart and in the hearts of my community. I may not see the fruit of such choices immediately, but there will come a day when the good fruit is harvested. What a glorious day that will be!

Climbing above the clouds, my eyelids grew heavy. Despite my tiredness, I felt a renewed hope in God. I know I'm too often bent on selfishness and self-destruction. To choose good goes against my nature, yet it's something the Spirit of God empowers me to do.

Thankfully, God not only provides the seed, but he also waters it and shines light on it. Scripture is quick to assign credit for the harvest to the work of God rather than mere circumstance. In the book of Genesis, the years of feast and famine foreseen by Joseph are attributed to God. The underlying message is that the God of Abraham, Isaac, and Jacob is in charge of the harvests—not a fertility god of Egypt. Despite this truth, all too often I give credit to happenstance or fail to acknowledge God at all.

I don't want to live this way anymore.

God, grow the reality of who you are in me, I prayed as I nestled my head into the headrest and drifted off to sleep.

PART III 🐝 The Land of Milk and Honey

3.1 | Discovery

My best friend and husband, Leif, introduced me to Cross Bar X Youth Ranch in Durango, Colorado, a few years ago. While we were dating, Leif kept telling me about this special place where he served as a counselor for three summers. For him, the camp was a place of joyful service as well as a sanctuary for personal restoration and healing. Shortly after we were married, Leif heard the camp needed a caretaker for a weekend so the staff could take a midsummer retreat. He jumped at the chance to return, and I went with him.

The once-emerald grass that covered the surrounding valley had turned hazel in the hot, arid weather. As we rounded the gravel driveway into the camp, I was struck by the sight of this vibrant oasis in the midst of so much sun-dried beige. Cushiony grass carpeted the fields, ending abruptly at the edge of a handful of lodge pole cabins. Horses stood at attention in their corral, waiting for riders. Hoping for a tasty treat, goats and sheep poked their noses through mesh gates. Against the faded, dusty background of the valley, Cross Bar X represented a place of hope and life. The camp workers were abuzz with activity. They were scrubbing, washing, watering, and finishing up all the chores that needed to be done after a busy week of camp.

Sporting a deep tan and a friendly smile, Nick, the founder of the camp, welcomed us into his home and introduced us to his wife, Tracy, and their four daughters. Over the course of the evening, I learned more about the camp, but what I found most intriguing was Nick's approach to ministry. He began three decades ago with a vision to reach low-income youth and has stayed true to that vision. He commits his life, his family, his resources—his everything, really—to fulfill that purpose. Absorbing the stories Nick and Tracy shared with us, I knew that for many of the kids at camp, Cross Bar X was the highlight of their year.

Over the course of the weekend, we watered and fed animals, weeded, swept, sorted, scrubbed, cooked, and cleaned—and we still went to bed each night with a long to-do list. The camp staff worked hard, but they knew how to laugh and play too. When they came back from their staff retreat, Leif and I were ambushed with water balloons. I knew we'd be back.

Since that first trip together, Leif and I have returned to Cross Bar X many times. When we heard that the camp was going to be short on counselors for a week in the summer, Leif and I packed for the six-hour drive from Morrison to Durango to volunteer.

We met campers whose fathers were under court order not to see their children because of abusive behavior. Many kids were living in broken homes, foster care, and centers for abandoned children. One child sat down to a lasagna dinner and announced, "This is the best day of my life!" simply because he had been served a hot meal. Another broke into tears because he knew that at the end of the week he had to return home.

During the evenings, we sprawled out on Nick and Tracy's comfy blue couch and high-backed chairs around the fireplace. With the cascading sound of the homemade waterfall just outside the front door, Nick asked, "What's next on your pilgrimage?"

"This one is definitely more challenging," I said. "I think I want to spend time with a beekeeper."

"Intriguing, but why?"

I explained that as I was researching, I couldn't help but notice the different agricultural images in the Scriptures. The references to bees and honey were far fewer than those of sheep and shepherds or farmers and fields, but I was still curious about their significance.

"Have you ever been around a hive before?" Nick asked.

"My mom was a beekeeper for a number of years," I responded.

"Really?" Leif said, intrigued by the detail. "How did I not know that?"

"My mom has managed to shoehorn a wide variety of experiences into her life," I explained. "She's worked in the surfboard industry, taught skiing and snowboarding, sold real estate and jewelry, taught elementary school, and even earned her sixty-ton boat captain's license. She's hard to keep up with."

"Like you?" Leif chuckled.

In elementary school, my parents moved from the sunny beaches of Florida to the Smoky Mountains of North Carolina. They designed and built a home for themselves on a hilltop near the Blue Ridge Parkway. The surrounding forest transformed into a glittering natural jewelry box of gold, amber, and amethyst in the fall.

Never one to sit still, my mom took an interest in bees. She traveled to a nearby town to purchase three hives, a stack of wooden frames, and a white beekeeper's outfit. Like most of the hobbies she pursued, she bought supplies first and read the instruction booklets later, learning as she went.

Not too long after my mom came home with her beekeeping paraphernalia, she discovered a beekeeper's best friend: a smoker—a metal can designed to be stuffed with paper or leaves or other kindling. When ignited, the can releases a thick smoke that pacifies the bees during opportune times, like when their honey is being taken. I can still smell the smoker when I think about my mom and her hives.

"So it's not just a biblical interest but a personal one too," Nick observed. "Will you spend time with your mom and the hives?"

That wasn't possible. When my parents left the Smoky Mountains to move to Colorado, my mom sold the hives to another beekeeper. I needed to find someone else who didn't just know about bees but loved working with them.

"Durango happens to be the home of Honeyville," Nick said. "One of the suppliers is a friend of the camp."

Honeyville is a place Leif and I had visited on an earlier trip to Durango. I love all things Americana and can't resist pulling off the highway to explore touristy sites with odd claims like "The world's largest round barn," "Home of the two-headed calf," or "Largest rubber band ball in the world." My favorite detours often involve food, which is why we stopped at Honeyville a few years before. The factory store sold specialty honeys, jams, jellies, and sauces—all with free samples, of course. Not satisfied with the size of the samples, Leif brought a jar of chocolate honey back to Alaska, and it found its way into a number of delectable treats.

Nick explained that people from the neighboring communities had supported the camp in countless ways over the years, and one of his friends supplied the camp with honey. Nick offered to contact him. Later that evening, Nick handed me a used envelope with a scribbled number on the back.

"Gary said he'd be glad to see you, so just give him a call," Nick instructed.

Even after my experiences with Lynne and Joe, I felt hesitant about calling a complete stranger and inviting myself over to spend an afternoon together. Two days later I gathered the courage to pick up the phone and dial the number. Gary greeted me with a kind, older voice. I began introducing myself, but Gary interrupted me.

"When are you coming?" he asked.

"Would tomorrow morning work?"

"Ten o'clock," he answered.

I hung up the phone, even more nervous than when I dialed. I had met Lynne once before the trip to Oregon, and our relationship had context—even if it was limited to a chance conversation ten years earlier, and, of course, I had known Joe for years. But now I was driving more than an hour by myself to meet a complete stranger to talk about bees and the Good Book. That evening I was hit by a fear-quake as Leif and I walked down the rutted road to our cabin.

"Leif, what am I doing?" I asked.

"You're being Margaret," he answered with a smile. "And I love that about you."

With the outdoor light of the cabin illuminating Leif's face, I found comfort in the gentle blue eyes of my best friend. I'm used to Leif towering above my five-foot-six-inch frame, and in moments like this his bulk is a source of security. He extended his arm around me and pulled me close to his chest.

"What if the time with Gary doesn't go as well as the time with Lynne?" I asked.

"You'll be fine, honey," Leif said with a grin. "Remember?"

"I love to choose my own adventure," I said without a hint of enthusiasm.

"You're going to come back with some great stories," Leif assured me.

I prayed he was right.

3.2 | One Man's Passion

The hour-long drive to Lewis, Colorado, was nothing short of spectacular. Nestled in the San Juan Mountains, the land is a slow-brewed blend of rolling hills, rugged peaks, and rocky crests.

Turning left onto a dusty gravel road, I looked across the sun-cured field and saw a wide white barn standing nearly a quarter of a mile from the side of the road. Potholes jarred my car, reminding me to slow down. Each side of the narrow road boasted sage-colored fields; hay bales rested across the acreage like brown rice sushi rolls.

As I neared the barn, a man with steel-colored hair and tan skin wearing a long-sleeved blue shirt, khaki pants, and leather boots greeted me on a four-wheeler.

"You Margaret?"

I nodded.

"I'm Gary," he said. "Ma'am, follow me this way."

Parking his vehicle near the entrance to the warehouse, Gary pointed me to a shady spot to park. I whispered a quick prayer for courage, stepped out of the car, and followed him toward the warehouse doors.

"Just looks like it's locked," he said, unlatching the lock and flinging the door open. Before my eyes could adjust to the darkness, my nostrils flared at the sticky sweet smell of honey.

The scent filled my lungs. Spying the wide opening, bees darted through the air, entering and exiting the warehouse with the speed and efficiency of attentive shoppers at a Black Friday sale at the mall.

"Are you afraid of bees?" Gary asked in a gentle, grandfatherly tone.

"My mom had bees," I said, shaking my head, "but only a handful of hives. Nothing like this."

My eyes adjusted to the dim light of the building. Stacks of white and green wooden boxes that reached from floor to ceiling filled almost a quarter of the right-hand side of the warehouse. I instantly recognized the square boxes from my childhood. Each set of three boxes on top of each other formed a wooden cube which housed a single hive. Though a few rogue bees buzzed around, I was confident that the hundreds of stacked cubes were mostly empty, perhaps awaiting the arrival of new queens.

In the far left-hand corner of the warehouse, I counted more than two dozen fifty-five-gallon drums, along with a pile of lumber used to build frames for the hives. A stack of broken frames rested nearby, awaiting repair, while boxes of glass jars lined the wall.

"So what's your favorite kind of honey?" Gary asked.

"Chocolate," I said without blinking.

Gary chuckled. "What's your favorite natural honey?"

His question disarmed me. I had never thought about the nuances of honey, let alone been to any sort of honey tasting, though the idea sounded delicious. Unsure of what to say, I pulled a rabbinic move and answered his question with a question.

"What's your favorite honey?" I asked.

"Well, it's definitely a personal preference thing, like chocolate or vanilla," Gary explained. "I'm not a fan of citrus honey, because after you swallow it there's an aftertaste to me, but other people love it. My favorite used to be black button sage from California, but I haven't had it in years. Right now, clover is my favorite."

At that moment, I realized that even though my mom had been a hobby beekeeper, I had a whole lot to learn about this honey-making business! When I later had the opportunity to study more about the flavors of honey, I found that there are more than three hundred unique types of honey available in the United States. Some of the more intriguing flavors include blueberry, buckwheat, eucalyptus, and orange blossom.

"So, Nick tells me you've been doing this for a while," I offered.

Gary's face perked up as I tapped into his passion: beekeeping. With boyish delight, he shared how he had started beekeeping as a hobby nearly forty years ago with fifty-three hives. He eventually decided to take the plunge as a full-time beekeeper, purchasing two hundred hives. He had barely made it through his first winter when he discovered the new hives were full of disease. At his peak, he had thirty-two hundred hives with an average of seventy-five thousand bees in each. That's nearly a quarter of a billion bees!

Spending time with someone who is passionate about their work (or faith) is contagious, and though some of the specifics Gary shared about the hives were overwhelming in detail, I found myself carried along by his enthusiasm.

"These the hives?" I asked, pointing to the stacks of boxes.

"They're hives, but they're not active," Gary explained. "You wouldn't want to be in here if they were."

He reached his calloused hand toward one of the wooden boxes, running his fingers along the edges of the inch-wide frames. The panel he extracted was lined with the darkest honeycomb I had ever seen. Most of the individual cylinders of the comb on the panel were empty, but those in the middle still had their "lids," which sealed in the gooey sweetness.

"Why is it so dark?" I asked.

Gary walked over to another hive and extracted a newly constructed frame that held a golden, thin sheet of wax impressed with tiny hexagons. He explained that the new frame always starts with a golden hue as the bees construct the honeycomb, but that as the waxy cylinders age, they darken.

"But they're still good?" I asked.

"The honey out of these tastes just as sweet as the new. It's from the clover that's in this valley," Gary said, holding both panels side by side. "Let me show you."

He pulled out a pocketknife, popped open one of the blades, and skimmed the lids of wax off the aged frame before scooping an index finger full of dark honey and pressing it against his tongue.

"Try it!" he urged.

I mimicked his action, delighting in the overpowering sweetness. Though the honeycomb appeared ancient, the golden droplet tasted as fresh and delicious as ever.

"Touch anything around here, and you can't help but get sticky," Gary said. "Let me help you." He led me toward a porcelain sink and invited me to rinse off my hands. It was obvious that he was going out of his way to make me feel comfortable, and I was grateful for his thoughtfulness.

"What's through there?" I asked, my curiosity piqued by a door on the side of the warehouse.

"Let me give you a tour of the place," he offered. "I want to show you where this all begins."

Though well into his sixties, Gary had an unmistakable liveliness about him. I followed him to a pile of lumber on the floor, where he explained that he had built and repaired most of the wooden frames and boxes (also known as "supers") over the years.

"You see all those frames?"

I nodded.

"That's a lot of splinters," he said, deadpan.

I couldn't hold back a smile as he led me back toward the stack of hives. After the frames are constructed, Gary explained, each needs a starter sheet of wax. A thin layer of wax is inserted into each wooden panel like a photo into a frame, and that becomes the foundation for building the wax cylinders. Placing his hand firmly on top of one of the wooden boxes, Gary was unable to hide his passion: "These are some of the most incredible creatures you'll ever encounter!"

Gary explained that each box contained a colony of between fifty- and seventy-five hundred bees. Yet despite so many inhabitants, there's only one queen, and her whole purpose in life is to lay enough eggs to keep the hive going. After the queen hatches, she goes on a mating flight with the drones. In that single flight, she'll be impregnated with enough sperm to lay eggs each day for the rest of her life.

"She's got to be the busiest stay-at-home mom ever!"

Gary unleashed an ear-to-ear grin. "What's really amazing is that if the queen knows that several other queens are about to be born, she'll leave and take a portion of the hive—tens of thousands of bees—with her to start a new hive."

"Queen bees are a possessive bunch," I said.

"Extremely," Gary attested. "But it's not because they want control over the hive, like their title might imply. It's just that a queen's sole purpose is to reproduce."

"So she's a baby maker," I said.

"Yes, and she can't allow anything to get in the way of reproducing," Gary added. He explained that when several queens are about to hatch in a hive, the first uses its stinger to poke holes in the individual cylinders where the other queens are, so that she is the only one that survives. On the rare occasion when two queens are born at the exact same time, they'll duel each other to the death.

"Because a hive can only have one queen bee?" I said.

"Exactly," Gary affirmed, proud of his new student. "It's the way God designed them."

I was intrigued that Gary was the first to bring up any mention of God. I could tell by the excitement in his voice that he was sincere. Here was someone who recognized the divine fingerprints on his work, and I couldn't wait to find out more. But I was still trying to wrap my mind around the process of making honey.

"Where does the honey come from?" I asked.

"The flowers," Gary said. "They provide the nectar, a sugar-filled liquid that bees drink and carry back to the hive, where it's mixed with an acidy secretion and left to brew."

"Like beer?" I asked, imagining bees hoisting tiny glasses of Honeycomb Hefeweizen.

"Not quite," Gary said. He explained that bees drink the sugary nectar from flowers and then take it back to the hive, where they repeatedly ingest and regurgitate it—ew! Because of the nectar's high sugar and yeast concentration, the bees have to lower the liquid's water content by fanning their wings to prevent it from fermenting. The reduced water increases the level of sugar, thus preventing fermentation. Finally, the bees place a wax cap on each full cell so it will ripen.

"Then you steal from the bees?" I asked.

"Yes ma'am, but not all of it," Gary explained. "You can't be greedy."

Gary pointed to a set of three boxes stacked on each other. Pointing to the top box, he explained that good beekeepers only take the top box. The bees need most of what is in the bottom two boxes in order for the hive to make it through the winter.

"Without these," Gary said, tapping on the lower two boxes, "they'll die."

3.3 | Beautiful Intricacies

My eyes caught a glimpse of several bees hovering just outside of the exit hole. While other bees came and went, they seemed to stay in one position, always oriented outward. When I asked Gary about it, he explained that those bees were guarding the stash of honey.

"But the hive isn't alive," I protested.

Though this wasn't an active hive, the bees still knew that remnants of honey remained, and they were determined to salvage every last drop. The hole in the side of the box served as the only entrance and exit to the sweet bounty inside. These custodians were doing their job of guarding the golden treasury for other members of their hive.

"How many different roles are there to fill within a hive?" I asked.

Gary explained that there are three types of bees: a queen who rules the hive, the drones who fertilize the queen, and the female worker bees.

The queen lives for around three years and can lay more than a million eggs in her lifetime. During peak breeding season, she can lay more than two thousand eggs in a single day—which, interestingly, is greater than her actual body weight.

Meanwhile, the drones don't do a lick of work. These slacker bees don't search for a single patch of rich nectar or pollen; their sole purpose is to mate with the queen during her maiden flight. Once this is accomplished, they become a burden on the colony, and they're eventually booted from the hive. Yet despite their single focus, they play a key role in the hive's survival.

The female worker bees make up the vast majority of the hive. During the height of summer when they're working nonstop, their lives may be as short as six weeks; but in late autumn, when there's no new brood being raised or nectar harvested, they can live up to six months. The type of work a female worker bee performs can change regularly.

Female worker bees are natural multitaskers. During their life cycle they perform all kinds of roles, from "nurse bees" who feed the older and younger larvae, to "fanning bees" who keep the hive cool, to "queen attendants" who feed and groom the queen. Among these workers, there are those who feed the drones, seal the honey, build the honeycomb, pack the pollen, and carry water.

Two of the roles that stirred my imagination were the "mortuary bees" and the "guard bees." The mortuary bees are not grim reapers bringing death, but tiny undertakers removing it. I imagined bees with black capes flying around removing the dead bees and failed larvae from the hive. Their work prevents disease and enables cells within the hive to be recycled.

The guard bees, which I had seen outside the hive with Gary, are the soldiers of the colony. Some of the bees hang out near the entrance and attack invaders or thieves who try to steal from the hive. This troop works tightly with the entrance guard bees, whose sole purpose is to inspect the incoming bees to ensure they're fulfilling their mission of bringing back pollen and nectar. They also monitor the scent of those who enter the hive to make sure they're members of the colony. Meanwhile, another troop of bees hovers around the hive to monitor any disturbances or threats.

As Gary commented on the various roles in a hive, I realized that bees and followers of God have something in common—each has a specific role to play in order to effectively serve a greater purpose within the community (and it might change).

I thought of the passage that describes some as apostles, prophets, evangelists, pastors, and teachers, as well as the Scriptures that examine various spiritual gifts. At times, we may be tempted to look at other roles in the church with derision or envy, yet a beehive is a physical reminder that every role is essential to the survival and strength of the whole.

We have a friend who works for a local church. During a time of cutbacks, his job was going to be eliminated because no one could really define or identify what our friend did. He couldn't even put his own job into words. Yet as the leaders reviewed his indefinable role, it was clear that he was a person who connected all the different ministries and generations in the church. He was the glue, the bridge, and while such a role is hard to express in a job description or to measure in an annual review, the leadership concluded that they couldn't afford to let him go.

When a church, like a hive, is filled with people working and serving in the roles God has given them—in a rich blend of uniqueness, responsibility, and unity—what amazing sweetness naturally abounds!

3.4 | Sudden Loss

Crouching beside a beehive, I placed a hand on the cold cement floor and lowered my eye to the level of the exit hole. This close to the wooden boxes, I imagined the hive fully alive, with layer upon layer of honey hidden from sight. I could almost feel the buzz in my bones.

Gary invited me to follow him into an adjacent workroom, where I was again overpowered by the sweet smell. A large machine snaked throughout the room. Gary explained how this honey processor automated the extraction of the honey from the frames, separating the wax and producing pure honey.

"This is where it all comes out," Gary said, pointing to a faucet on the side of a huge tank. I was surprised that so much activity could be boiled down into a stream flowing out of something that could have been part of my kitchen sink.

While looking at the processor, a bee landed on my lower arm. I made eye contact with Gary, then looked back down at the bee, who seemed more concerned with finding a place to rest than a person to sting.

"Just stay still, and she'll fly away," Gary advised.

I knew he was right. The worker bees foraging for nectar or pollen only sting when handled roughly, and the guard bees only sting when they believe their hive is threatened. I took a close look at the tiny creature with whom I shared a truce. A thin layer of velvety fuzz coated the bee's jellybean-shaped abdomen, which was lined with alternating stoplight-yellow and pitch-black stripes. Two thin, wiry antennae protruded from above the bee's hook-shaped nose, while its goggle-like eyes seemed to take in everything. After about ten seconds, the bee flew away.

"Where do you store the honey?" I asked, relieved that I was no longer a landing pad.

"That's where the drums come in."

I followed Gary back to the main room of the warehouse, where he stopped in front of the collection of fifty-five-gallon drums.

"These shouldn't be empty," he said with an unmistakable sense of loss in his voice.

His sober tone reminded me of something I'd been reading about: Colony Collapse Disorder. Bees have been dying in record numbers, and the impact has extended far beyond the borders of the honey industry.

Unbeknownst to the bees, in the process of searching for nectar and collecting pollen, these insects transfer pollen from plant to plant, fertilizing the plants and enabling them to bear fruit. Estimates suggest that one-third of the human diet is derived from insect-pollinating plants, and the honeybee contributes 80 percent of all pollination. So this issue is personal.

Some of my favorite fruits and vegetables are dependent on the busyness of the bee. Without bees, the production of avocados and almonds, cherries and cranberries, strawberries and squash, peas and peaches are all affected. The balance of our ecosystem is threatened by the loss of bees, and the impact eventually affects farmers everywhere—including my friends in Nebraska.

What caught my imagination as I read about the seriousness of the situation is how such a small creature could have such a huge effect on the world. Beyond the few wild hives nestled in a rock on the hiking trail behind our home, I rarely encounter beehives. I may see a stray bee while enjoying an afternoon in the park or inspecting a patch of fresh flowers, but generally these creatures seem inconsequential to my life.

I took a second glance at the empty drums and gently asked, "Have your bees been dying too?"

"We've lost almost everything."

Gary explained that three years ago, he and his son had twenty-two hundred hives and lost nine hundred of them in a single winter. The next year, they lost seven hundred more. Last winter, they lost less than eighty. "Every year you'll lose some hives, but usually it's just a handful, not almost half your bees," he said.

"What do you think it is?" I asked.

Gary thought for a moment and knocked his knuckle against one of the empty barrels, releasing a hollow clanking sound that hung in the air. "We have four main bee labs in the US, and they're all researching this issue. We're hearing that the losses are from a virus in the bees that's been around for years, but this particular strain is producing giardia-like problems. When the virus gets in the gut of the bee, the lifespan is dramatically shortened."

The real issue, according to Gary, wasn't the bees dying as much as the timing of their deaths. "The problem with bees dying is that the majority of bee losses are happening in the winter," Gary explained. "So none of the bees in a hive are surviving until spring. Entire hives are being wiped out in a two- to three-month period."

Gary shared how a few years before, he and his sons took their hives to California in preparation for the almond blossoms. Almond growers need the bees to pollinate each flower for the nuts to grow, so they pay beekeepers to bring hives to their orchards. On New Year's Day, the hives looked fine, but a month later the hives collapsed. More than three-quarters of the bees died.

In an effort to save the hives, they transported the bees to Texas where they could experience an early spring and have a chance at survival. The expensive move paid off, and Gary was able to save some of the hives.

"So you've been rebuilding?" I asked.

"We ordered six hundred queens this year. We had a good winter with lots of moisture, and the extra water supply made everything want to bloom, but we ended up having the worst dandelion season in years so there were few flowers for the bees to gather pollen from. We've already lost two hundred of the queens."

A wave of empathy crashed over me. I could tell the years of loss were taking a toll on my new friend. We stood in the barn, side by side, in silence.

"You just have to adjust to what you're given," Gary eventually said. His tone revealed he had paid a price to own this truth.

Gary pointed to the RV parked in front of the barn. "We were going to let my son and his wife and our grandkids build a home on our property here, but after the collapse, we decided to move into a Fifth Wheel RV and give the kids our home. Maybe in a few years things will rebound."

Before I met Gary, the loss of bees was only something I had read about in the newspaper or watched on the news. But now the loss had a face and a family. The cascading ripple of cause and effect was simple: without bees, no pollination or honey. That whole cycle was summed up in one life: Gary's. Gary had been pursuing his passion for more than forty years. Like a tree blackened by lightning that still buds in the spring, Gary held out hope for better days.

As we stood together, I watched a pair of bees zigzag into the

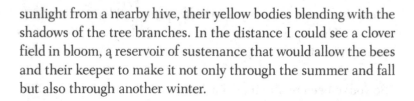

sunlight from a nearby hive, their yellow bodies blending with the shadows of the tree branches. In the distance I could see a clover field in bloom, a reservoir of sustenance that would allow the bees and their keeper to make it not only through the summer and fall but also through another winter.

3.5 | Bees of the Bible

Though I didn't know where Gary saw himself in the spectrum of faith, he invoked God's handiwork when he described the intricacies of the hive. I couldn't help but wonder how working as a beekeeper flavored Gary's belief in God. Did he see things in Scripture that I could not, simply because of his profession? Did he interpret passages differently because of what he knew about bees? Or the trials he faced?

I followed Gary into the one area of the warehouse we had not visited, a shed mounted against one of the walls. He had purchased the prebuilt shelter from a local hardware store a few years before in response to his wife's need for an area to pursue her candle-making hobby. What began as a pastime became integral to their business. With heavy imports from China, the price of honey dropped to such an extent that the couple had to tap into secondary revenue streams from the hives like pollinating almond trees in California and creating handmade beeswax candles for gift shops. Gary described the radical change in the industry without a hint of bitterness; he had merely adapted.

A series of wooden shelves on the left side of the shed held the metal castings used to create the candles. While a few sat empty, most were filled with a creamy yellow wax, a white wick hanging limply at the apex of each one. Gary grabbed one of the molds shaped like a honey bear and pried it open. Once the excess wax was trimmed from the edges where the two halves of the mold met, the wax bear candle was ready to be packaged. A wick emerged from between his round ears, though I couldn't imagine anyone lighting the cute little guy.

The shelves on the opposite side of the shed boasted a rich collection of completed candles in ornamental shapes, including crosses, corn, honeybees, wild bears, pine cones, and an assortment of globes. Behind the candles I could see grandkids' finger-painted artwork lining the wall.

Gary explained that the beeswax is a substance secreted from the female worker bees and used to build the honeycomb where the honey and pollen are stored. Beeswax doesn't come without a cost. In order to produce one pound of wax, a bee must consume sixty pounds of honey.

Grabbing two dusty metal chairs and pulling them beside the worktable, I unpacked my well-traveled Bible. While I discovered nearly seven hundred references that involved sheep or shepherds in the Scripture, and half as many that involved farming and fields, less than seventy mentioned bees and honey. Yet honey appears consistently throughout Scripture. Maybe it's my love of food, but the presence of honey in the Bible serves as a tangible reminder that the truths of Scripture are a multisensory experience.

One of the most popular sweeteners in history, honey is a rich, nutrient-filled food mentioned in the Old and New Testaments. Even though bees are the ones who make honey, God is portrayed as the One who provides the honey. Nearly two dozen references throughout the Old Testament describe the Promised Land as a place "flowing with milk and honey." This first appears in God's conversation with Moses in the presence of the burning bush.

David and his people receive honey (among other foods) while surviving in the wilderness and hiding from Saul. Jeroboam's wife takes cake, loaves, and a jar of honey on her travels. Honey is even

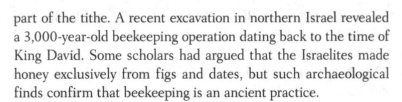

part of the tithe. A recent excavation in northern Israel revealed a 3,000-year-old beekeeping operation dating back to the time of King David. Some scholars had argued that the Israelites made honey exclusively from figs and dates, but such archaeological finds confirm that beekeeping is an ancient practice.

The first time honey is mentioned in the Bible is in the story of Joseph. After his adventures—which include being thrown in a pit by his brothers, doing time in jail for a crime he didn't commit, and spending years in slavery—he finally rises to the position he has been destined for all along: he is ruling over the land of Egypt. When he sees his brothers after decades, he keeps his identity hidden and sends them back to get the missing brother, Benjamin. When Joseph's father, Israel, hears of the ruler's demand, he tells his sons to pack their bags with the best offerings of the land as gifts to appease the ruler. These include spices, pistachio nuts, almonds, silver, and honey.

Thus, the first time honey is mentioned, it's part of a gift to win favor. Israel instructed his sons to take "a little," possibly signifying the specialness of the honey.

God promised to bring his people out of Egypt into "a good and spacious land, to a land flowing with milk and honey." The promise of a "good" land highlights the land's fertility, while the promise of a "spacious" land offers a sharp contrast to the tight living quarters the Israelites had experienced under the oppression of the Egyptians. The promise that the land would overflow with "milk" suggests abundant pastureland for goats and cows, while the mention of "honey" implies that the land was abounding in flowers and grass. Such a detailed portrait of a promise reveals something about the outrageously generous heart of God. He didn't just want to end slavery for his people. He wanted to bring them out of the land entirely and into a new place that overflowed with provision.

Even on their way to the Promised Land, during that difficult time in the desert, God gave his people a taste of the better things that were to come. He provides sweet manna for them. This heaven-sent food has been compared to coriander seed and is described as tasting like wafers with honey.

When the Israelites finally arrived at the border of Canaan, they sent spies to evaluate the situation. The scouts confirmed the abundance of the land by noting that it flowed with milk and honey. This observation became one of the Promised Land's defining characteristics, even though the land could have had other descriptions. According to Deuteronomy 8:7–9 and 11:10–12, the land also boasted produce, including wheat, barley, pomegranates, fig trees, vines, and oil. So why did milk and honey become the trademark description of the Promised Land?

Some scholars suggest that milk was one of the most important staples in the Hebrew diet next to bread. Any land that boasted excess milk and honey had to maintain extensive pastures, which meant plenty of water as well—important when you've spent time in the desert. Or perhaps honey was viewed as a luxury, and thus a land with milk and honey could meet both one's needs and desires. Some scholars suggest "milk and honey" may be an example of Hebrew merism—the literary use of opposites to cover the spectrum of everything in between—reminding the Israelites that the Promised Land contains absolutely everything in abundance.

3.6 | Overflowing

I read God's promise of this overflowing land aloud to Gary. He held up his hand in protest.

"You know I'm not a theologian," he said.

I assured Gary that I wanted his perspective as a beekeeper, and his posture relaxed.

"Well, then," he paused, "speaking *just* as a beekeeper, a land overflowing with honey is naturally bountiful, a land that's got everything you need and then some."

He explained that in ideal conditions, a hive of bees will collectively travel as far as 55,000 miles and tap more than two million flowers to make one pound of honey. A productive hive can make up to two pounds of honey in a single day. Many natural factors affect the bees' ability to make honey, including the amount of seasonal rain, the variety and abundance of vegetation, and the type and frequency of weather patterns. To Gary, the mention of honey meant all these things had to be in place, a perfect gathering of good things in the land.

"You do what you can to protect the hives and give the bees the best possible chance for a good year, but in the end, God is the one behind the control panel," he observed.

Gary was not just a man of faith, but a man who had held on to his faith in all the roller-coaster ups and downs of beekeeping: the years of battling disease among the hives, the years with too much rain or not enough, the years when the flowers blossomed in wild abundance and those when buds grew scarce. The yield of his honey had been affected by everything from drought to heat waves, late to early snow, and even changes in native plant life. For Gary's land to overflow with honey, the right conditions had to align perfectly.

That's why the detail of the Promised Land overflowing with honey was so important: God promised his people a land where everything was in top working order. This was a land abounding in fruitful pastures and efflorescent vegetation. This was a land functioning in its proper, God-designed rhythms. The result was natural abundance. The description "overflowing with honey" offers a glimpse into what God desires and promises us all—an invitation for us to taste and see that the Lord is good.

3.7 | Insights of the Hive

I set the scene of one of the Bible's riddles from the book of Judges that involves honey. I shared with Gary the story of Samson killing a lion. A few days after the encounter, Samson passed by the carcass of the dead animal and discovered a beehive inside the cavity. Samson turned the encounter into the famous riddle, "Out of the eater came something to eat, and out of the strong came something sweet," which no one solved until Samson's wife betrayed him in order to get the answer (Judges 14:14).

"Could this really happen?" I asked. "Would wild bees build their hives in a dead animal?"

"Bees can make a home in almost any hole," he explained. "I've seen bees in hollow trees, stumps, and even in cliffs. Bees always need a place to store their honey. That's what causes them to swarm."

Gary explained that a swarm is a group of bees that have left a hive. Swarming is crucial for the survival of the species. As soon as a colony of bees fills its hive with honey, it swarms and forms a new colony. When there's more honey than the hive can contain, it's time to divide and multiply.

"Can you catch a swarm?" I asked.

According to Gary, swarms sound scary but there's nothing to fear. Since swarms don't have honey or a young brood to protect, they're generally benign. He said the easiest way to catch a swarm is to find one on the limb of a tree. He described finding a ball of living bees on limbs. The weight of the swarm weighed down the limb, so all he had to do was flick the branch and they fell into a box for him to take away and put into a prebuilt home.

"I've seen swarms the size of grapefruits all the way up to pumpkin-sized swarms," Gary said, expanding and contracting his hands to various sizes. "As long as you get the queen in the box, the rest will follow."

That explained how the bees had gathered inside the decaying lion. A swarm had probably formed and moved inside the nearest cavity it could find.

I noticed that a honeybee had landed on the table and seemed to be content eavesdropping on our conversation. When I tapped my fingers on the counter, the insect took flight. As the bee disappeared into the shadows, I asked Gary about another passage that piqued my interest. In 1 Samuel, there's a story of one of Saul's blunders as a leader. When the Israelites engage in a battle with the Philistines, Saul orders his people not to eat until they declare victory or they will be put to death. Saul's son, Jonathan, doesn't hear the order and, entering the forest, discovers "honey on the ground." Seeing the honey, he takes his staff, dips it into the honeycomb, and enjoys the sweet nourishment. Only then does a soldier inform Jonathan of his father's decree.

Though Jonathan openly admits his error, Saul is merciless. The death penalty remains in effect. The people come to Jonathan's rescue—defending him to his own father—and save his life.

My question for Gary concerned the honey on the ground. "Would bees," I wondered, "ever produce honey on the bare ground?"

Gary furrowed his brow in deep thought. Holding up a single index finger, he paused for a moment. "Heat could cause that," he finally said.

He picked up a piece of paper, outlining it with his index finger.

"If this is a frame from a hive and it's full of honey, then the only thing supporting that honey is the wax—those six-sided cylinder shapes," he explained.

Like a kind professor, Gary explained that the design of the honeycomb was brilliant, since a hexagon is one of the strongest shapes. Yet even with the six-sided construction, higher temperatures will affect the strength of the wax.

A hive needs to stay below ninety-six degrees. In order to maintain an optimal temperature, bees create their own air conditioning system. On hot days, bees go out and fill up one or both of their stomachs with water. When they return to the hive, they regurgitate the water and then fan their wings over the water to cool the hive. But a problem arises when bees don't have access to enough water to maintain the temperature of the hive.

"Since wax is the only thing supporting the heavy honey, it will naturally start to sag under the heat," Gary said, "which would account for the honey running onto the ground."

Reflecting on Gary's insight as a beekeeper, Saul's order to his soldiers seems all the more foolish and cruel. Perhaps his armies had been fighting in hot weather with limited access to water. Sending people to fight under those conditions was another reminder that Saul had let the crown go to his head and lost compassion for his people and those who fought for him.

3.8 | Sweet Words

Knowing that Leif was waiting for me back at Cross Bar X, I turned to the next passage tucked in the book of Proverbs that describes pleasant words as a honeycomb, sweet to the soul and healing to the bones.

I wondered about the idea of healing, knowing that a few friends had touted honey for medicinal purposes.

"Does honey or a honeycomb have any healing properties?" I asked.

"Honey has all kinds of vitamins in it, and it's one of the most healing things I know," Gary said.

Often when he's working with the frames of hives, Gary elaborated, he'll get splinters or cuts in his hands, but in more than four decades he's never had an infection when working around honey. He has even used honey to help heal burns.

"If me or any of the grandkids ever got a burn, we'd slather it with honey and wrap it loosely in a bandage. The air can't get to it, and something in the honey causes it to heal rapidly," he explained. "And when you eat honey from your local community, you're consuming the pollen from local plants, so your body builds up a tolerance that helps with allergies."

Some of the scientific literature I read confirmed what Gary described. Honey is considered an antimicrobial agent, which inhibits the growth of certain bacteria, mold, and yeast. Its high sugar content and acidity, as well as the presence of hydrogen peroxide in low concentrations, are believed to help treat minor skin injuries. Before the advent of antibiotics, soldiers in battle would use honey to help dress their wounds. The antimicrobial properties of honey helped to prevent infection, and the stickiness of the honey helped makeshift battlefield bandages to remain in place.

In my research, I was intrigued by the mention of royal jelly, a substance I had seen advertised for its health properties. The substance is a secretion from hypopharyngeal glands used to feed all the larvae in the colony.

What's fascinating is that if a hive needs a queen, then a single larva is selected. This chosen one will receive royal jelly only for its first four days of growth. The rapid, excessive feeding on royal jelly triggers the development of a queen, including the ovaries she needs to lay eggs. The hive was a more intricate place than I ever dreamed!

Honey is a sign of healing and abundance throughout the Bible. Yet I couldn't skip by the passages that reversed the symbolism. The prophet Isaiah predicts to King Ahaz that a promised child, Immanuel, will eat curds and honey. Though Ahaz may have understood the words as a prediction of blessing and abundance, the foretelling turns dark as the prophet predicts that the land will be invaded, the crops destroyed, and vines devastated. Survivors will live on whatever they can find—including honey, which transformed from a sign of abundance to a symbol of judgment and loss for the nation.

Honey is also significant for other biblical prophets. When John the Baptist arrives on the scene in the New Testament, his diet—which includes wild honey—is representative of his raw appearance and message. John the Baptist's story has parallels with Elijah, the prophet of old who called a nation to repentance. Both men's lives and lifestyles were physical manifestations of the spiritual realities they were calling people to embrace. Surviving on wild honey (and locusts) was a physical portrait of depending wholly on God for provision.

I reached down and ran my finger along the edge of one of the frames that rested nearby. I brushed the gooey substance against my thumb and raised it to my tongue, remembering that the psalmist described the laws of the Lord as "Sweeter also than honey and the drippings of the honeycomb" (Psalm 19:9–11). The fresh honey

tasted like liquid candy, and although my mind swirled rapidly around the deliciousness of the moment, I wanted my heart to hold on to its taste as a lasting reminder of all I was discovering.

3.9 | The Faith of a Beekeeper

As our time together came to a close, I had one final question.

"How has working as a beekeeper for all these years affected your faith?" I asked.

Gary paused for a long while before answering. In the stillness I could hear the humming of fluorescent lights, and I watched as bees darted through the air.

"If I put on the beekeeper's protective clothes and took someone out to the hive, then sat down with them and pulled the frames, explaining how it all works together, I think it would be hard for the person to leave without acknowledging that God was involved," Gary said. "So many things have to come into play before those bees make one drop of honey."

Though some might dismiss Gary's faith as simplistic, his expression and countenance revealed that he had discovered something unmistakably holy in his work. Through his time with the bees, Gary recognized the great lengths God goes to provide for all his creatures. He recognized the hive as well-organized and designed. Through the honeycomb, Gary witnessed the wisdom and beauty of God. He also discovered just how much God loves even the smallest of details.

As I packed up my Bible and notes, Gary handed me a jar of honey. I promised to savor every last drop.

On the drive back, I found myself scanning the fields for flowers and young buds, those details blossoming in my consciousness. I was even appreciative of the stream that wound its way beside the ribbon of road, recognizing the precious life it sustained. All were crucial in the balance of nature for the bees' survival.

That afternoon I discovered that a subtle but significant change had taken place in my own heart. I found myself increasingly in awe of our God who pays attention to the minutest details.

Some people excel at seeing the big picture and identifying overarching themes and goals. Others specialize in the particulars—the fine-tuning of systems and functions. But God is not like us. He specializes in everything, from pollen patterns to distant galaxies. God knows when a bee doesn't make it back to its hive. He numbers the wing beats it takes to create a single drop of honey.

An enormous amount of work, planning, and design go into creating honey. How much more goes into God's Word? Surely it is no accident that the shepherd-king who spent years roaming fields compared God's Word to honey in Psalm 119:103. If so many complicated details are orchestrated by God for a bee to produce one drop of honey, imagine how much more attention to detail God has given to every word of Scripture!

Such overwhelming attention to order and detail reminds me that God cares for us more deeply than we can possibly know. All too often I read Scriptures like Jeremiah 29:11—which says that God knows the plans he has for us, plans to give us a hope and a future—with a kind of been-there-done-that attitude. Over the years, I've read, heard, and seen those types of passages so many times that their depth has evaporated. I'm confident in my mind that God has a plan, but in my heart I can't help but wonder.

Inside the hive, I catch a glimmer of how everything comes together for good. God is able to orchestrate what seems like nothing more than a swarm of buzz into a productive, healthy source of nutrition and sustainability. God has created the bees to work together for a common good. A hive is a portrait reminiscent of Paul's vision of the body of Christ: although we are gifted differently, our purpose remains the same. Is the church much different? Should the church be any different?

If a community of bees can do so much with so little, how much more can you and I accomplish with the great resources our Father has given us? Bees face countless challenges with variances in weather, wind, and vegetation, yet with diligence they produce something that cannot be manufactured any other way. Real honey has no substitute, and neither does the body of Christ.

As I pulled back into the driveway of Cross Bar X, I watched with delight as two boys tugged at the long legs of a counselor, trying to wrestle him onto the soft grass. Like the bees, each staff member was hard at work. All were committed to a single cause—ensuring the campers enjoyed one of the best weeks of their life. By the end of the week, I knew they would be exhausted and spent. Yet like the bees, each was part of a small, recurring miracle.

"How was the time with Gary?" Nick asked.

"Sweet," I said without cracking a smile. "Thank you for introducing us."

After dinner and Leif's evening lesson with the campers, I sat with some of the counselors recounting the events of the day while sipping a cup of vanilla peppermint tea laced with orange blossom honey. I had never appreciated the distinctness of the honey before—the light color, hint of citrus, and fresh scent. Without realizing it, I had discovered my favorite honey. Tasting the liquid sweetness, I found myself infused with a renewed hope in a God who is in control of even the tiniest details.

PART IV   The Vine

4.1 | The Hidden Vintner

Maybe you know lots of vintners, but when I started researching, I didn't know any. Where exactly does one find a winemaker? I mentioned my desire to spend time with one to family, friends, and acquaintances, but no leads turned up. While many of them had visited vineyards—and a few offered to tag along as research assistants!—none knew a vintner personally.

I wanted to find someone who had some sort of biblical framework in their background who could appreciate Jesus' first miracle—turning water into wine—and Jesus' frequent use of a vineyard as the setting for his parables. Six months and a trip to Fresno, California, later, I was still looking for someone who could provide deeper meaning into the Scripture. No one seemed able to help. No one, except for Cathleen.

While catching up with my dear friend on a red couch, slightly stained, in a coffee shop in Chicago, I mentioned my need to her. "This shouldn't be that hard," I said, taken aback by the exasperation in my own voice.

"My friend is a master vintner in Napa Valley," Cathleen said nonchalantly.

"You're kidding me!" I said. "Do you think he'd let me come visit him and hang out?"

"Let me Facebook him and find out."

By the end of the day, I was electronically introduced to Kristof, and he graciously extended an invitation to visit Napa to learn more about his work. We scheduled a time in late February when the fields would be dormant, and he would have a few afternoons to spare.

Leif, Hershey (yes, we brought the dog), and I touched down in Sacramento in the late afternoon. The first thing I saw in the airport was a wine store. Just as Vegas is crammed with slot machines at every turn, this gateway city to wine country promised we wouldn't travel far without running into grapes, vines, or a famous bottle of wine.

That evening we enjoyed the hour-plus drive toward the valley as the sun melted on the horizon. By the time we saw the signs for Napa, the silhouettes of the surrounding low-rise mountains were illuminated only by moonlight. Though the scene was beautiful, I longed for what daylight would bring.

Morning did not disappoint.

Our ten o'clock drive to meet Kristof was a breathtaking immersion into a world I like to call "greentopia"—a land where lime, sage, jade, chartreuse, shamrock, and olive all come out to play. The valley was prodigal with vegetation. The surrounding hills boasted lush trees, a sharp contrast to the pedicured vineyards below.

Each plot of land had been staked out. Though every owner had a different method—some used wooden stakes while others used metal, some vines' tendrils reached into the air while others had nothing more than stubs—each vine had been painstakingly nurtured and handcrafted to stand at attention in precise rows that looked like above-ground electric lines. Vineyards blanketed the face of the ridges like a patchwork quilt.

4.2 | Wine Country

Leif followed the directions to Gargiulo Vineyards, a small-scale, boutique Napa Valley vineyard where Kristof consults as a master vintner. A thin sign marked the address of the private label vineyard and estate. We followed the gravel road around a bend, where we discovered Kristof eating his lunch out of a plastic to-go container in the center of the circular driveway. Wearing a plaid, short-sleeved shirt, a vest with an embroidered logo of a wine barrel that read "Trust," and light blue jeans, Kristof had the expression of a kid with his hand in a cookie jar.

"You caught me eating my lunch," he said between mouthfuls. "But you can park over there."

He pointed to a paved area on the side of the brown stone and stucco building overlooking the vineyards below. The large warehouse had a modern design with clean lines, and from the driveway I could see tidy rows of barrels and large steel processing equipment inside.

"What's for lunch?" I asked, unable to make out the remains of Kristof's bowl.

"Emergency Top Ramen," he said. "I always keep a few on hand."

I smiled. If Napa was known for its outstanding wines and gourmet food, then I was being given a backstage pass, ushered behind the

scenes where the regular people live. The lack of presumption immediately endeared Kristof to me. Anyone who eats Top Ramen standing in the middle of the driveway is a friend of mine.

"I know a great place we could talk," Kristof offered.

Leif and I followed him into a building lined with huge storage tanks and aging barrels. The smell of red wine, thick with berry, vanilla, and oak, filled my nostrils. The area was directly linked to the winery's greeting and tasting area. We followed a narrow hallway decorated in warm tones, accentuated by a silver bowl of fresh granny smith apples resting in the windowsill.

The main room was decorated in modern southwestern chic. Oversized leather chairs surrounded a thick dark wood table. Unshelled pistachio nuts rested on a sterling platter, tempting those who passed by. Four guitars lined the wall, ready to be plucked down and played by visitors looking for a place out of the sun. We climbed a spiral staircase in the center of the room to an upper sitting room with built-in couches on every wall. A few round metal tables rested in the middle with fiery red flowers propped at an angle in square glass vases. Along the edge of the ceiling, a special shelf had been built to hold unlabeled, backlit wine bottles. The lighting and soft orange hue transformed the glass containers into works of art.

"How did you end up here?" I asked, settling into one of the pillows, fluffy, hand-stitched, on the couch.

Kristof explained that his grandparents had moved from Sweden to the United States and settled in California. He was raised with a European upbringing and developed an appreciation for fine food and wine early on. "In European culture, it's normal to drink wine with dinner and on special occasions," he said. "It's something I grew up with."

His culinary appetite whetted, he decided to pursue a career as a chef, but at the last minute was persuaded by a family friend to consider medicine. Kristof studied at Wheaton College outside of Chicago. During his sophomore year, he was challenged by an assignment to investigate a denomination outside of the Protestant one he knew. He visited an Orthodox church and was taken by the steady grace of its millennia-old liturgy. Around the same time, he switched his major from premed to earn a double degree in business and art and fell in love with a young woman named Jennifer who shared his last name.

"So I went to Wheaton College to become a doctor and ended up becoming a winemaker, embracing Eastern Orthodoxy, and meeting my half-Swedish, Californian wife with the same last name," Kristof said with a hearty laugh. "It's not your typical evangelical story."

"I love it!" I said, unable to hide a huge grin.

"Your bag is moving," Kristof observed hesitantly.

I had forgotten all about Hershey. Unzipping the mesh bag, I pulled out my soft charcoal dog.

"He sure is quiet," Kristof said.

"We like it that way," I said, slipping him back into the bag.

Kristof explained that after graduation, he and his girlfriend (now wife) returned to California, where she enrolled in graduate school at UC Davis. That's when Kristof took a map of the area and drew a one-hour's drive radius around the school to begin looking for employment. Kristof contacted a family friend who had started a winery in Napa. "He didn't need anyone and neither did the next guy, but over the course of that week, after following a laundry list

of recommendations, I was hired as a bottling supervisor," Kristof recalled.

"How did that go?"

"I didn't know the first thing about a winery, but since I had a college degree and was willing to work hard, the winemaker took notice, and I became a cellar rat," he recalled.

"Is that a promotion?"

"More of a lateral move," Kristof explained. "Cellar rats hook up hoses, clean things, and perform the hands-on labor that winemaking requires. In a kitchen, it would be equivalent to a prep cook."

After that first harvest season, he became a "flying winemaker" and traveled to South Africa for their fall harvest season. When he returned to Napa, Jennifer was barely speaking to him because of his long absence, and he knew that if he wanted to make the relationship work, he had to find more permanent employment in the valley.

He worked for a handful of wineries before landing a job in a premier wine lab, where he studied enology (ee-nol-uh-jee)—the science of wine. Eventually, he moved up to be the assistant to the head winemaker. In 2001, he created his first vintage. As a winemaker consultant, he now makes wine for four different labels.

"So you're a master vintner?"

"You could call it that, but no one really does," Kristof explained. "Just a vintner."

"Okay, vintner," I repeated.

"Many of these artisanal vineyards aren't large enough to hire full-time employees and instead choose to rely on highly experienced contract labor and professionals," Kristof explained.

"Like this winery?" I asked, pointing out the window to the vineyard below.

"Exactly," Kristof said. "And I love the size of it, because basically I'm a chef who grows his own ingredients. By being small, I'm vertically integrated. In other words, nothing happens at any stage of the winemaking where I'm not involved in the decision."

"You look at every vine?" I asked.

"Not only that, I look at every cluster of grapes—at least once, but probably two, three, or even four times."

"That's a lot of tender care," I observed.

"That's what it takes to be a good vintner."

4.3 | A Craftsman

"What do you love most about winemaking?" I asked.

"I love that what I do is tied directly to weather and seasons," Kristof said. "There's a continual year-long cycle to what I do with the grapes, but there's also a longer cycle for the wines as they age."

"In some ways, you're an artist," I said.

"I prefer the word *craftsman*," Kristof clarified. "Making wine engages me on so many levels—in chemistry, microbiology, mathematics, linear and abstract thinking. While it may not be considered as creative as other professions, I still think it's a craft."

"Because it's never the same," I suggested.

"Never!" Kristof said. "One of the things I enjoy about wine is the fact that it's new every time. Even if the bottles are from the same barrel of the same harvest, every time I open one there's something different."

"So it's new every morning," I said.

"Well, hopefully you're not drinking it in the morning," Kristof quipped.

The image I had of Napa Valley as a place of recreational gourmet play was a far cry from real life in the valley. I wondered what surprised people most about the region.

"People are sometimes disappointed to discover that winemaking is nothing more than glorified farming," Kristof admitted. "I started before six o'clock this morning, and I put in long hours throughout the year. If it weren't for the fact that we were fermenting grape juice into really great wine, no one would come to Napa. No one goes around visiting multi-million-dollar chicken sheds or corn farmers to see how they farm."

I appreciated Kristof's honesty but couldn't help but wonder what had made Napa, well, Napa. He explained that back in the 1950s some far-sighted farmers placed strict "no growth" measures on the land. As a result, the property rose in price and demand. In addition, the climate was naturally complementary to wine growing, and after local winemakers began winning tasting competitions, demand for Napa Valley wine skyrocketed. Though the region produces less than four percent of the wine in California, Napa has become synonymous with winemaking and is the second-most-visited location in the state behind Disneyland.

"People love this place!" I said.

Kristof smiled and described a wine dinner he hosted a few years earlier. A Supreme Court justice sat across the table from Kristof and talked the entire night about winemaking. "I'm with a justice from the US Supreme Court, and he couldn't stop talking about wine," he recalled. "I'm sitting there with mud on my boots and realizing this guy just wants to be doing what I'm doing. How crazy is that?"

4.4 | The First Sign

Jesus' miracle in Cana is fascinating. Unlike most modern weddings in North America, marriages in ancient Israel were celebrated as week-long feasts. This required a significant commitment by the family, who served large quantities of food and wine.

From the description in John 2, Jesus' mother Mary was likely a friend or relative of the bride or bridegroom, and Jesus had been invited to the feast with the disciples. On the third day of the wedding—a note that hints at the third day of the resurrection as well as the banquet prophesied for the end of time—the wedding hosts are out of wine. This was not simply embarrassing to the families of those being married, but a crisis of honor and an unexpected financial expense.

At this moment, Mary turns to her son for help. Undeterred by Jesus' protest—"Woman, what does that have to do with us? My hour has not yet come" (John 2:4)—Mary tells the servants to blindly obey whatever Jesus commands.

Jesus asks the servants to fill six stone ceremonial jars with water and then take some to the headwaiter. Somewhere between the dipping and the palate, a miracle happens: common water becomes choice wine.

The pronouncement by the headwaiter that this wine should have been served earlier testifies to the wine's quality. When Jesus performs this miracle, he bypasses the restrictions of time. As Kristof later explained, producing wine takes years, beginning with prepping the soil, then growing and pruning the vines, harvesting the grapes, collecting the juice, and finally fermenting. When it comes to making great wine, time is your friend. Yet Jesus didn't need to wait.

Jesus' first miracle is also intriguing because he is not just fulfilling an immediate need or responding to his Jewish mother's insistence. John describes the act as a "sign" (Greek *semeion*) rather than "a miracle" (Greek *dynamis*). The word choice conveys that the act was disclosing something about God that had previously been hidden: that Jesus is the Son of God radiating the power and presence of his Father.

"What strikes you about the story of Jesus turning water into wine?" I asked.

"Some people think that serving the best wine first is only an issue of sobriety, but it's also smart because of the tannins in wine," Kristof explained. "Tannins are what cause that dry, puckery feeling in your mouth similar to biting into a green pear. They impede one's ability to taste. To appreciate the flavors, the best wine should always be served first.

"The other thing that strikes me," Kristof continued, "is that the story gives me a greater appreciation for winemaking in ancient times. Knowing the difficulty of making fine wine, even with all our modern technology and science, it's easy for me to discount the perceived quality of wine consumed in biblical times. I just kind of assumed it was a simple-tasting drink. But for the headwaiter to acknowledge the host's wine selection implies a high level of sophistication of the people and their palates in those times, which gives even more weight to the role of vineyards and winemaking in various passages."

4.5 | Long-Term Investment

I asked Kristof if we could see the vineyard. We followed him out a side door onto a gravel path. Red stone walls lined our steps. Vineyards rolled into the distance, as far as the eye could see.

Land in Napa is nothing you can afford to waste, and the edge of the vineyard was only a stone's throw from the front door. The vineyard stretched down a slope before leveling across the plain. Each row revealed a stout, inverted L–shaped vine. Planted equidistant from each other, the vines simply reached up with a solo branch running parallel to the ground. All other signs of growth had been removed.

"It looks dead," I said.

"You should see it in four weeks," Kristof pushed back. "You wouldn't recognize this vine, it will be so green and alive."

I brushed my fingers against the dry flaky bark, struggling to imagine this vine containing any life.

"Let me show you," Kristof said, pulling out a pocketknife. He scraped one of the nubs on an offshoot of the vine until a light green bud appeared.

"But it looks so dead," I said. "If this wasn't a vine in your care and you stumbled upon this in a random field, would you know whether it was alive or dead just from looking at it?"

"I wouldn't know," Kristof admitted. "You have to go below the surface to tell."

I paused for a moment to reflect on the spiritual insights Kristof was inadvertently giving me. I wondered if he realized the profundity of his simple observations.

"So what does it take to grow a healthy vineyard?" I asked.

Kristof explained that a good vineyard always begins with preparing the land—removing the rocks and trees, along with their underlying root systems. Soil preparation involves amending the ground for nutrients before the stakes and wires are installed. Then a dormant shoot from a grapevine or a young growth from a nursery is planted. At the end of the year, it's pruned all the way down to two buds on the cane.

"Basically, it looks like you cut off all the growth," Kristof explained. "The owners usually freak out at that stage."

"At what point do the owners stop freaking out?" I asked, tongue-in-cheek.

"They never stop freaking out!" Kristof grimaced. "Anyone who farms worries because they know something can always go wrong. With a winery, more money is involved, and whenever there's more money, people become more worried."

I looked at the gnarled vine, and then at the surrounding estate. With a Napa Valley vineyard costing an average of $60,000 per acre to plant and $6,000 an acre to farm every year after that, I calculated the costs mounting. No wonder worry crept in.

Though the annual expense of the vineyard decreases after the first year, caring for the vines is constant. Kristof explained that it's during the second year that the vines are especially micromanaged. Each vine is pruned to grow in a way that will establish it as a healthy base for decades to come. Finally, in the third year the vine is permitted to reach up to the trellises and produce a modest amount of fruit. Each year after that, the vine is carefully sculpted, or pruned, as it grows. Without consistent care, the vine will create abundant fruit but with little meaningful flavor.

"When does a vintner get to taste the first wine?"

"This is a long-term investment," Kristof answered. "The third year, we get some fruit, but we let it drop to the ground. The fourth year, we'll get a small first harvest, which is fermented and aged in a barrel for two years before being bottled. Between the first planting and the first bottle is about eight years."

"I had no idea."

"That's something people new to the valley really fail to appreciate," Kristof affirmed. "In this industry, you're not making your first dollar until year eight, and you're probably not making a profit until year fifteen or twenty."

"And the whole time you're keeping an eye on the vines and the wines?"

"Making wine is like making a reduction sauce," Kristof said. "If you walk away to answer the phone, you could lose the whole thing if the fermentation process goes too far."

"So you always have to be ready?" I asked.

"I have a cot ready to sleep nearby so I can keep a close eye on the wine for bottling," Kristof said. "And on more nights than I can count, I've used it!"

4.6 | Girdling

The previous fall Leif and I had traveled to Fresno, California, to see extended family. While there we drove through the valley's abundant farmland and spent time with a farmer who sold his produce —including grapes—to outlets like Delmonte (raisins) and Gallo (wine). The vines we saw in Fresno were different—not just because harvest was nearing—but also because of the actual vines. Each vine was six to eight inches at its sturdiest point, a far cry from the mere one to two inches we looked at in Kristof's vineyard. In addition, each of the Fresno vines had scarring in the form of rings around the base of each plant. Some had as many as two dozen lines around them.

When I asked a farmer about the scars, he called it "girdling" and explained that the vines are cut each year in a circle around the base. The cuts convince the vine to pull more nutrients from the soil and produce a higher quantity of fruit. If a vine is girdled too deeply it will die, but if the cut is just right, the same plant will produce twice as many grapes.

Explaining what I had seen in Fresno, I asked Kristof why he didn't girdle his vines. The answer had to do with the quality of grapes he was producing. In Fresno, many of the vineyard owners push their vines for highest productivity, whereas in Napa Valley, vintners were looking for best quality. While a one-acre vineyard could comfortably produce between ten to twelve tons of grapes annually, Kristof's vineyard only produced one to two tons of grapes each year—almost ten times less. The result was a grape with more intense and multidimensional flavor and aroma.

I thought about different pastors and congregations I know and saw a parallel. Some churches gather thousands and they're highly productive in the number of people they reach. But other churches are more like Napa Valley vineyards. They may be small, but the character, the depth, the unique flavor of Christ within the community is unmistakable. While some might be tempted to disparage one growing style over another, both have their place.

Kristof's BlackBerry hummed, and he graciously dismissed himself to a meeting with the promise that we'd see each other again the following afternoon at another one of the wineries he worked with.

We said our goodbyes and enjoyed a leisurely drive back to our hotel, stopping in downtown Napa to visit a few antique stores and grab a quick bite. I was excited to see what the next day would bring.

4.7 | Sonoma

Kristof called the next morning to give us directions to the vineyard in case the rural address was too remote for our GPS. Little did he know our GPS, nicknamed "Bianca" and sporting a trustworthy British accent, rarely failed us.

I scribbled down his directions anyway and promised to be there by eleven o'clock. Driving toward Sonoma, the road was lined by a light green Easter-basket grass so vibrant it looked almost plastic. As we passed into Sonoma County, I saw my first Oreo cow—the thick white stripe around its black body triggering a craving for cookies and milk.

The address was posted on a tiny wooden sign that we almost missed, but thanks to Bianca's matronly tone, we made the sharp right-hand turn. We followed a long gravel road to a house on the side of a hill surrounded by oak trees. While the building was more modest than the one we saw the previous day, the landscape was just as spectacular with its acres of vineyards and slow-rolling hills.

Kristof popped out of his truck wearing an Australian outback hat, a brown fleece vest with the insignia of Demptos (another barrel company), a plaid shirt, and the same worn jeans and brown boots he'd sported the day before.

He welcomed us warmly into the building, which had been transformed from a home into a series of offices and meeting rooms. The sparse décor included a handful of built-in shelves with wine bottles, a wooden table with six metal chairs, and a stack of back issues of *Wine Spectator*. The design was simple and functional.

We sat down and began talking, but my stomach was grumbling. "Any chance we could go grab some lunch?" I asked.

Kristof took us to Vineburg Deli, which boldly claimed the best BBQ tri-tip steak sandwiches around. I couldn't resist. Leif opted for a BBQ half-chicken. Surrounded by the wealth of food options, I was a bit surprised when Kristof ordered an ordinary egg salad sandwich.

"It's just what I order when I'm here," he said. "It's what I like. And I'm here a lot during harvest season."

Unpacking our lunches back at the winery, he disappeared into a downstairs room and returned with a barebones yellow bottle that simply had a cork and sticker on the side.

"This is what we produce here," he said.

"How would you describe it?" I asked.

"This is buttery lemon, zesty, with a hint of sweet oak," he said. "It's got green apple, as well as a bit of under-ripe pear."

I was amazed that he could put into words the flavors that electrified his taste buds. As much as I wanted to taste the wine—and oh, how I wanted to have the flavors bubble on my tongue like Kristof described—I knew that some who heard of my experience would be bothered, disturbed, or disappointed if I took a sip.

I felt a war brewing in my gut. One inner voice encouraged me to drink, reminding me that the taste was part of the experience, an essential element of my journey. Another inner voice reminded me that such an act would come at the cost of alienating others. Those who had experienced the abuse and addiction of alcohol and stood firmly against drinking would be pained by my decision. Resisting the urge to taste and tell, I listened to Kristof's description and reminded myself that sometimes loving others is about what you do, but more often it's about what you leave undone.

Looking around at the barebones operation, I couldn't help but contrast everything I had seen in Napa against what I was experiencing in Sonoma. Kristof confirmed my suspicions.

"There's a definite rivalry between Napa and Sonoma—especially when it comes to winemaking," he said. "Napa tends to be more upper end with huge estates, whereas in Sonoma, you'll see more of the farming community. The Sonoma locals joke that Sonoma is where you go for wine and Napa is where you go for auto parts."

4.8 | Wine in the Bible

In between bites of grilled tri-tip, I asked Kristof about two books that he had brought with him. He explained the thin red volume was an Eastern Orthodox book on prayer, and the second was an Orthodox commentary on Scripture.

I had prepared for my time with Kristof by scouting the nearly two hundred mentions of vines and vineyards in the Bible—no surprise, since Israel is a land of vineyards. Just as the Israelites looked forward to the Promised Land as being a place overflowing with milk and honey, they were also expectant that it would have lush areas to plant vineyards. In fact, two of the spies brought back bunches of grapes that were so heavy they had to be carried on a pole between the two men.

Like sheep and shepherds, vines and vineyards provide a backdrop to some of Scripture's most memorable stories. While in a vineyard, Balaam and his donkey encounter an angel, and Elijah's fiery showdown with the prophets of Baal takes place on top of Mount Carmel, a place that can be translated "vineyard of God."

The prophet Isaiah portrays Israel as God's vineyard, a land and people that he loves and has gone to great lengths to plant, cultivate, and protect. Like the image of God as a shepherd, the description of God as a vintner is one that implies a great investment of time, energy, and care. It also implies the expectation and promise of a fruitful and abundant harvest.

If God's people are compared to a vineyard, it should not be a surprise that at times the Bible condemns the vineyard for its scarcity of fruit and characterizes its fruit as rotting. The prophet Jeremiah uncovers Israel's estrangement from God by exposing their choices to pursue worthless idols and vain efforts to support themselves. God asks, "Yet I planted you a choice vine, a completely faithful seed. How then have you turned yourself before Me into the degenerate shoots of a foreign vine?"

The prophets often draw on this image of a vineyard producing bad grapes in order to paint a portrait of God's judgment. Even though the vinedresser does everything possible to grow luscious grapes, if the vine only produces bad fruit, then the vinedresser will have no choice but to destroy it and plant a new vineyard.

Another reference to the judgment of God is described when the vineyard produces good fruit, but the people will not be able to enjoy the harvest. In Deuteronomy, those who break God's laws may plant a vineyard but not enjoy the fruit. Zephaniah draws on this image when he proclaims that the people of God will not be able to enjoy the fruit of their labors because of their sin. This is used both figuratively and literally, since military invasions often resulted in the destruction of agricultural production for a community. It was not uncommon for enemies to plunder and destroy the crops of the conquered land.

While the loss of the vineyard is a sign of judgment, fruitfulness is a sign of God's restoration and redemption as well as his promise and blessing. God makes it clear that one of his blessings is that his people should enjoy the fruit of the vine both in eating and drinking. Grape juice naturally ferments to produce wine, and while Scripture clearly forbids drunkenness, the fruit of the vine remains a promised source of enjoyment for God's people.

The abuse of this enjoyment provides some of the most colorful illustrations of foolishness in the Bible. Though vines were most likely found in the garden of Eden, the first time a vineyard is mentioned is after the flood. Noah, who is described as a man of the soil, was probably not the founder of viticulture, but he certainly appreciated its fruits. After emerging from the ark, one of his first courses of action is to plant a vineyard. He foolishly drinks the wine until he passes out. His youngest son, Ham (the father of Canaan), finds him in his tent, naked, and rather than cover up his father, he tells his two brothers. Shem and Japheth walk into the tent backward to cover up their father without looking at his nakedness.

When Noah discovers what his youngest son has done (or left undone), he curses Ham's descendants, Canaan, to be the lowest of slaves. One of the things that is particularly interesting (and depressing) about this story is that Noah—who has himself felt the grace of God in the covenant to never again flood the earth—curses one of his own grandsons.

Drunkenness brings out the worst in God's people. Lot commits incest with his daughters while drunk, and the kings Amnon and Ben-hadad are killed while drunk. King David tries to get Uriah drunk to cover up the Bathsheba incident. Leaders who drink too much often compromise justice and morality. Proverbs warns listeners to stay away from drunkenness and all the foolish delusions and decisions that come with it.

Alongside these clear warnings to stay away from drunkenness, the

Bible draws on the image of the vineyard as a source of provision and blessing, a reminder that admonitions against over-enjoyment don't prohibit proper, and God-ordained, enjoyment. When Jacob blesses his two sons, Judah and Joseph, he describes Judah as tying his donkey to the best branches of a vine and having his robes washed in wine. Meanwhile, Joseph is described as a "fruitful vine." This particular description is intriguing, because a vine was also part of the dream that the chief cupbearer had that Joseph interpreted.

In the New Testament, the vineyard becomes a representation of the kingdom of God. Jesus weaves vineyards and vines into his stories, and in one of the most well-known teachings he describes himself as a vine, inviting us to remain in him in order to produce fruit. Jesus uses the fruit of the vine on the evening of his arrest as part of the final meal that his followers are told to repeat in remembrance of him. These were the kinds of passages I couldn't wait to unpack with Kristof.

4.9 | Restoration

Over lunch, I pulled out my Bible and read several different passages to Kristof, imbibing his wisdom and words. One of the more intriguing was Exodus 22:5, which pronounces, "If a man lets a field or vineyard be grazed bare and lets his animal loose so that it grazes in another man's field, he shall make restitution from the best of his own field and the best of his own vineyard."

Did such a guideline have any connection to the world Kristof lived in?

While he was quick to point out that roaming animals weren't a threat to vineyards in the valley, he had heard about a plane accident that destroyed portions of a field where vines were valued at two thousand to three thousand dollars each.

"I like that the Scripture clarifies that you're supposed to give the best of your vineyard when you make restitution," Kristof said. "When we plant new vines, we cut off canes or portions of older vines to start the new ones. God would have us choose the best part of our vineyard, because in reality you could give someone an area you knew wasn't the best, like a vine infected with virus or one of the weak vines."

From Kristof's simple observation, I had another minor epiphany of sorts, namely that the Exodus passage wasn't just meant to guard people's vineyards but also their hearts, since they might be tempted to make restitution with something less than their best.

I bit into a piece of tender steak, allowing the peppery flavor to melt on my taste buds. Wiping the corner of my mouth with a white paper napkin, I asked Kristof about another instruction found in Exodus, that every seventh year the land should rest and lie fallow. The Scripture is specific in saying, "You are to do the same with your vineyard and your olive grove" (Exodus 23:11). In fact, when God spoke to Moses at Mount Sinai, he spoke directly about this issue of allowing the land to have a sabbath (Leviticus 25:1–6).

Kristof explained that while it's harder than ever for vintners to follow this advice, the longer you leave a parcel fallow the better it is for the next vineyard you plant. Since the vines are taking nutrients out of the soil, the longer you don't plant vines, the more the soil can restore itself. This is true not only when you plant a new vineyard but also between series of harvests.

"The downtime allows the soil of the vineyard to regain the nitrogen it needs to produce a delicious harvest," he explained. "The trick is maintaining a balance of fertility in the vines. Overly stressed vines will struggle and produce fruit of lower quality for wine. Excessively happy vines will be too prolific and create thin, uninspired wines."

Unknowingly Kristof had touched on something I had been learning in my own spiritual life. Just as the land needs a sabbath, I do too. Over the last few months, Leif and I had been on the road traveling, teaching, and researching. Most of the commitments had been made more than a year before, long before we had learned to calculate recovery time into our trips. The result was go-go-go without any chance to rest or recover. Not only did I find myself catching every strain of flu that went around because of a weak immune system, but I also struggled with irritability, overeating, and overreacting. I felt discombobulated and out of balance. As we were nearing the end of our busy time, I discovered the sweet moments of life were losing their savor, and the sharp moments were growing more bitter.

Life without the gift of rest is merely existing without being able to enjoy the bouquet of all we have been given. Just as the fruit of Kristof's vines eventually suffered without respite, so did the fruit of my own life.

Kristof finished the last bite of his egg salad sandwich, which struck me as an odd companion to his glass of chardonnay, but he didn't seem to mind. He glanced at his watch. "There's supposed to be a meeting in here in ten minutes, but we can move to a back office," he suggested.

We cleaned up the table and followed a narrow hallway to a bedroom that had been converted into an office. A single brown desk and chair and a blue couch with yellow checks filled the room, while a square beige-and-white rug tied the simple design together.

The only piece of artwork was a long, rectangular hunter-green sign that read, "Scribe. Sonoma, California," in an elegant platinum sans serif font. "Thought you'd like that," Kristof announced. "I think that's going to be the final label design. Regardless, that's the brand of wine we're producing here."

I liked the simplicity of the composition but loved getting a glimpse behind the scenes of the work involved in designing a single bottle. "So much work goes into this," I observed.

"It's constant," Kristof acknowledged.

His words provided the perfect segue into something else I wanted to ask. The vineyards I had seen in Napa and Sonoma were refined and highly cared for, but what about neglected vineyards? What about the vintner who is depicted as a "sluggard" in Proverbs 24? The Scripture describes passing by a vineyard that is completely overgrown with thistles and nettles, its stone wall broken down. Had Kristof ever seen such a thing?

Not to that extreme, but he acknowledged there are levels of quality when it comes to vineyards. Those who plant the vineyard often take the best care of the vines, because of the amount of time, money, and energy invested. But as vineyards are passed on, depending on who buys or inherits them, the quality of care can decrease.

"All too often the people who inherit the land don't have the same work ethic or ability as their parents," Kristof said. "There's a loss of appreciation for all they've been given and all the work that's gone into the land."

"So you've seen vineyards neglected," I clarified.

"Even in the prized growing region of Napa, I've been surprised by how some current or previous owners have opted to do things the cheapest or fastest way, while they have known the right way."

"What's the long-term cost?" I asked.

"When you don't tend a vineyard for a year, you suffer a lot of loss

and damage. It takes years to get it back in balance and to where you had it before."

Looking back, I see times in my life when I have let my relationship with God go—the weeds sprouting up and stealing nutrients, runaway branches taking away from my fruitfulness. God is faithful to restore, but like a vineyard, it takes time to bring things back to life and a healthy balance.

4.10 | The Proverbs 31 Vintner

I felt the sunlight filter through the milky windowpanes, warming my cheeks. As Kristof and I talked and Leif listened in, natural lulls in conversation emerged as I pondered what Kristof said. Yet these moments were anything but awkward. Because Kristof was comfortable with himself, he had a knack for making everyone around him feel at ease. I felt like I could ask him anything.

Reflecting on all that Kristof had shared, I was interested in one of the details regarding the woman described in Proverbs 31. Often hailed as the ideal woman, the Scripture tells us that one of the many things she does in her free time is buy a field and plant a vineyard. This passage is intriguing because of its context, coming after some strong words a mother gives her son about avoiding strong drink. Overindulgence leads to poor decisions about women and life, as well as apathy over caring for the poor. This contrasts sharply with the Proverbs 31 woman, who is specifically commended for her business acumen and care for the poor.

I read the final chapter of Proverbs aloud to Kristof. Of all the places she could invest her time and money, she selects a vineyard. After walking among the vines with Kristof and learning just how much went into growing grapes, I found the Proverbs 31 woman's choice a bit odd.

"Why?" I asked abruptly. "From your perspective, what's going through her mind?"

"She's resourceful, for sure," Kristof said. "But there's something more. Anyone who plants a vineyard is looking ahead to the future. She has the foresight to know that it's going to be three to four years before she sees any fruit—both literal and figurative—from her labor. But she also knows that for the fifty years after that, she and her family are going to get fruit, and even if it's not for wine, she's still thinking long-term. If you're only thinking for the here and now, you'd plant a different crop."

As I thought more about it, her foresight becomes even more obvious. Throughout the Old Testament, the image of growing a vineyard is one of stability, financial prosperity, and longevity. Maybe the Proverbs 31 woman knew that Solomon, too, had planted vineyards. It would take plenty of work, and I'm sure some sleepless nights, but her investment would pay dividends to her family for years to come.

4.11 | Laborers' Squabbles

Though I hadn't moved from my place on the couch, the shifting shadows of the sun reminded me that time was passing more quickly than I wanted it to, and Kristof had his work to attend to. Though he was more than generous with his time, I didn't want to take too much.

I transitioned Kristof into the New Testament. In Matthew 20, Jesus tells a parable of a group of workers who begin their jobs at different times throughout the morning and afternoon. All are paid the same amount. When questioned about the fairness of his pay scale, the owner of the vineyard reminds each worker that he agreed to work for a denarius. Yet it doesn't seem equitable that someone who pops in at the end of the workday should make the

same wage as someone who has been working in the hot sun for an entire day.

"What do you make of this?" I asked.

Kristof took in a deep breath and held it for an extra moment. The story reminded him of an issue he faces when paying his harvest workers. Different types of grapes and areas of a vineyard pick at significantly different rates, and the workers are paid based on the weight of what they pick. On a given day, one group of workers may work all day and earn one hundred dollars, while another group earns three hundred dollars.

"We are clear to tell the crews—especially those who don't get paid as much—that they'll switch areas tomorrow and the money will even out, but they get so angry," Kristof said.

"But that's different," I pushed back. "In the parable, God never says it will even out."

"True," Kristof said. "But the issue of jealousy is the same. In the parable and in the vineyards, there's squabbling among the workers. The jealousy is real. And in both cases the workers have to look to the owner or manager of the vineyard for resolution."

Kristof was right. While his workers could find resolve the next day, the resolution in my own life is less clear. Many others are sharing the gifts they have with the world in the same way I try to, but late at night I often wonder why they seem to attain more success with far less work or effort. At those dark moments when I find myself asking, "Why is this so hard?" "Why them?" or worse, "Why not me?" the vineyard owner is the one I must turn to and choose to trust—even in inequality, even in exhaustion, even when things don't add up.

I watched Kristof cover his mouth as a yawn escaped and knew that lunch was taking its toll. Quickly turning to Matthew 21, I read another of Jesus' parables rooted in a vineyard: the story of the two sons. One day a father asks his sons to go work in the vineyard. The first says no, but then regrets his decision and heads out, while the other son agrees to go but doesn't. Jesus poignantly asks which of the two sons did the father's will. The first son, of course! Jesus reminds us that tax collectors and prostitutes will be welcomed first into God's kingdom—if they, like the first son, feel remorse and act on it.

Kristof was quick to point out that vineyards are different than many areas of work because one can always measure productivity. "It's very visual and laid out," he explained.

"I can have a guy out there and calculate in ten minutes how much work he did, and then figure out how much he should accomplish in an hour and even an entire day. Most jobs aren't like that."

"How does that relate to the parable?" I asked.

"If the father went out to the vineyard that night, he knew immediately that his son hadn't been there. An area of the vineyard was untouched," he explained. "Odds are the sons were either pruning or picking, so the fact that the son lost a day is very measurable and has a lot of impact. In a vineyard, that's a day's worth of work you can't get back, so you're falling behind continually."

Kristof's observation tapped into an issue that I had often struggled with in my relationship with God; namely, *how much is enough?* If my life is like a vineyard, and if what I do (or leave undone) is measurable to God, then at what point does sleeping in or skipping work for a single day affect what God is doing in our world through me?

Yet is that an unhealthy question to ask? Do I really put that much stock in what I do, or is it more important to learn to abide in God and allow him to do his work in and through me? Such discussions remind me of the tensions of living a life of faith and trying to find the balance between faith and works. I tend to swing to one extreme or the other, and I need God to move me more toward the center.

4.12 | New Wineskins

Sitting in the back office, I paused for a moment to reflect on the amazing journey that had brought me to Kristof. I realized that the hunger inside of me to know God and know his Word only increased as we talked. Learning from someone who knew so much about vines and wine was adding a new layer of depth to stories I had read many times before. One of those Scriptures was a moment when Jesus commented on wine and wineskins. Though John the Baptist had come to announce that a new era of change was coming, a few of his disciples struggled with that change when it began to happen. They came to Jesus to ask him why they had to fast but Jesus' followers did not. Jesus answers their concerns by turning their attention to how they store wine.

When I asked Kristof about the use of wineskins, he explained that most were probably from goats. Unlike the modern barrels, ancient vintners would store their wine in tanned animal hides. These wineskins expanded as the liquid fermented until the skin hardened and became brittle. If fresh wine was added, the now inflexible wineskin would burst as gasses escaped, and both the new wine and the old wineskin would be lost.

In modern processing, wine still must have an outlet for the gasses it produces. This principle is as true today as it was thousands of years ago.

Jesus knew that many of his listeners believed the old wineskin (or way of doing things) was good enough. They were comfortable with their beliefs and practices, but Jesus hadn't come to patch up old religious traditions. He was offering a new garment, a new wineskin, a way of life that didn't abolish the old ways but fulfilled them.

The teaching illuminates my own need to remain pliable before God. I realize that I must have a softer housing for my growing faith, one that can flex and change as God is at work inside of me. All too often I find myself clinging to that which is comfortable and familiar, rather than embracing the challenges that emerge with change and growth. Sometimes I shy away from people who have strong views that differ from mine, even though sharing a great conversation over breakfast could temper both our viewpoints and deepen our relationship. Why do I run away from strong opinions and potential conflict? Am I too comfortable and unwilling to change? Such a realization highlights the need for the Spirit in my life not just to discern and distinguish, but also to illuminate and invite me to move forward into the fullness of life with him.

4.13 | The True Vine

Reflecting on Jesus' statement, "I am the true vine, and My Father is the vinedresser," Kristof released a warm *hmmm* sound before declaring warmly, "I love this verse."

I had been waiting to unpack John 15 with Kristof from the moment I met him. When I looked at his vines, I saw gnarled plants with crusty, brittle bark, clinging to life. The tiny buds sprouting underneath the rough exterior of the branches were waiting for an experienced pruner to guide their growth.

Reading through the passage in which Jesus compares himself to the true vine, Kristof noted that it was quite a metaphor. I asked him to look at the passage line by line through the lens of a vintner.

"What's interesting is that the passage doesn't identify the full role of his Father," he observed.

I was confused. The passage clearly said that the Father was the vinedresser. "What do you mean?" I challenged.

"In a vineyard, people often have multiple roles, and the Father probably isn't just the vinedresser—he plays a role as the owner of the vineyard, the manager of the vineyard, and the vintner too," Kristof said. "But of all the titles, Jesus gives his father the title of vinedresser, and that's the one who prunes or sculpts the vine."

I wondered why the role of vinedresser was so important. Why didn't Jesus give the Father the title of owner? While Scripture didn't say, Kristof had an intriguing observation.

"It may surprise you, but whoever is pruning a vine really is the master. Even in our vineyards, the owner may possess the land, and I might be making the wine, but it's the guy with the pair of shears making twelve dollars an hour who has all the power."

Kristof continued reading aloud, "Every branch in Me that does not bear fruit, He takes away; and every branch that bears fruit, He prunes it so that it may bear more fruit."

Pushing his chair back from the desk, he balanced for a moment on the back two legs and looked thoughtful. He explained that as a kid when he had read that passage, he always thought the practice of pruning was easy.

"I thought you'd just walk up to a vine, see a branch with fruit, and say, 'We'll keep that one,'" Kristof reflected. "You'd see another branch without fruit and cut it off. But as a vintner there's a lot more decision-making and expertise going on in this passage than appears at first glance."

"What do you mean?" I asked.

"It's the little cuts that are the most important," he explained. "You can't come in with a pair of shears and clip like crazy. You don't just look at what appears to be a dead branch and cut it off, and then look at a branch full of fruit and think it's fine. Over the course of pruning, you make a series of very precise, strategic cuts that will produce the healthiest, most robust vines."

"Which highlights just how intimately God is involved in our lives," I interjected.

"And also how God handles each of us differently," Kristof added.

He explained that if a vinedresser chooses the wrong cuts, the vine won't produce fruit. That's why a vinedresser looks at each vine carefully. Every vine is unique. Even two vines planted next to each other may require significantly different pruning in order to produce fruit.

"One vine may have great soil and be strong enough to handle a significant pruning, but the next vine may be weaker, and the same pruning would leave it fruitless," he explained.

"Which may be one of the reasons Jesus chose to describe his Father as vinedresser," I offered. "He's the only one who can make those judgments."

Hershey, who had been sitting quietly on my lap, stood up and looked at the door and then at me.

"I'll take him," Leif offered and disappeared out the office's back door, the cool fresh air wafting into the room.

I nudged Kristof forward in the text to the invitation of Jesus to abide in him. I read John 15:4 slowly: "As the branch cannot bear fruit of itself unless it abides in the vine, so neither can you unless you abide in Me."

Kristof didn't hesitate to respond. "What's interesting is that the branch (or cane) is what's used to plant a new vine," he said. "But if you cut off a branch and expect it to bear fruit on its own without a root structure or nutrients and water—it will simply wither up and die. The vine is the source of life. In the abiding, the fruit grows."

The last verse was the one that seemed to stump Kristof: "If you abide in Me, and My words abide in you, ask whatever you wish, and it will be done for you."

"That one has always bothered me," Kristof admitted.

"Why?" I asked.

"Because I've seen people use the promise 'Ask whatever you wish' to do some pretty ludicrous and even abusive things."

"I have too," I acknowledged. "But being here with you and walking the vines gives me hope in Jesus' words."

"How so?"

"Because the vines, your vines, are a perfect portrait of abiding. The vine is the source of everything for the branch—every nutrient, every life-giving drop of water, every hint of growth. The branch is completely dependent on the vine. But even in those moments when I grow wild or unbalanced, God is faithful as a vinedresser to perform all the small cuts I need to remain fruitful. So in that place where I am abiding in Christ under the watchful eye of the Father, I can trust that the Father will be pruning those areas and desires in my life that don't line up with where he wants me to go."

Kristof smiled. He rested his hand on the stack of paper on his desk that contained a list of the Scriptures we had discussed.

"May I keep these?" Kristof asked.

"Absolutely," I said. "I cannot thank you enough."

Leif returned with Hershey in tow. The pup leaped onto my lap and looked at my bag that served as his carrying case.

"Yes, it's time to go!" I affirmed.

"I want to give you something," Kristof offered. We followed him back down the hallway and into the lobby meeting area. Kristof disappeared and returned with a bottle of Cabernet. The label simply read "Pella" in calligraphy.

"Your daughter," I observed.

"My wife and I make our own label of wine, and we named it after our oldest daughter," he explained. "We only make four barrels—about twelve hundred bottles a year."

"I will treasure it," I promised. "Maybe I'll even share it with Cathleen!"

Kristof smiled. "Give her a hug for me."

4.14 | Until That Day

Saying goodbye to Kristof and the valleys of vinelandia, I found myself reflecting on all I had learned. I was grateful for Kristof's kindness and willingness to let me get a glimpse inside his work and craft.

As we drove past more vineyards than I could count, I realized how my faith had been stretched in my time with Kristof. I had learned so much about viticulture—the amount of time it takes to produce a glass of wine, the fine art of pruning, the precision required to make great wine—that I never knew before. I wondered how it would affect one of my favorite spiritual practices: Communion.

The institution of the Lord's Supper is one of the most meaningful rituals of the Christian faith. Eating his final meal with his followers, Jesus enjoys the aroma of freshly baked bread (sans yeast), the tang of pungent herbs, the pleasure of tasty meat, and the joy of sharing life through conversation with friends. The Gospel of Matthew tells us that "while they were eating" (Matthew 26:26), Jesus takes the bread, gives thanks, breaks off and hands out portions to his disciples, instructing them to take and eat. Then he takes the wine, again giving thanks, and serves it to his followers. Their palates alive with flavor, Jesus explains the meaning of his actions. Such a scene is starkly different from what I encounter when I take Communion at church.

Standing in line to receive a miniature plastic cup filled with watered-down grape juice and a flat, tasteless wafer is a far cry from the multisensory, communal experience that Jesus asked us to do in remembrance of him. While still a meaningful spiritual practice, I think at times I miss the relational aspect of Communion not just with God—but with my friends who love Jesus.

As I read the familiar account, I was reminded that in the shadow of Judas' betrayal, the unleavened bread became a stunning illustration of Jesus' body—broken and shared with those around the table. Together with the cup, they illustrated that Jesus was about to become the once-and-for-all sacrificial lamb.

The cup that Jesus raised was one of the four cups of wine that were part of the Passover celebration. Some believe that Jesus was raising the third cup, referred to as the cup of redemption, when he declared it to be his blood poured out for the forgiveness of sins.

I have a hunch that Jesus cherished every moment with his faithful followers on that final evening. It wouldn't surprise me if he savored every last bite and sip of the Passover meal, enjoying the tangy and bitter flavors that tasted not only of what was but of what is still to come—a foretelling of a meal and relationships that would last forever.

Yet it wasn't until I spent time with Kristof that the poignant promise of Jesus' declaration, "I will not drink of this fruit of the vine from now on until that day when I drink it new with you in My Father's kingdom" (Matthew 26:29), came alive. When Jesus lifted up his glass and made that final declaration, he was most likely lifting up the fourth cup of Passover associated with the promise of Exodus 6:7 (NIV), "I will take you as my own people."

I always thought the excitement regarding Jesus' return was on our part.

But what about Jesus?

He waits with even greater expectancy and passionate longing than I ever will. When he raised his cup, he was already thinking about the next time he would be with his followers. He was already anticipating the marriage supper of the Lamb, a meal that is the fulfillment of what the Passover and the Lord's Supper foreshadow.

As I sit down to a quiet meal in our home, my mind wanders to that promised meal in heaven. Our glass table in the kitchen easily holds a simple dinner of salad, rice, and chicken for the two of us, but it couldn't possibly contain the bounty that will be present in heaven. Who will I sit by? What conversations will I have? Will I

talk to the apostle John or a young woman from China who lost her life because she refused to deny Christ?

The Lord's Supper is also a reminder that, above all, God desires relationship with us—the kind of relationship that grows deeper through a lifetime and into eternity. Whether during walks in a garden or afternoon conversations, he wants to spend time with us, know us, and be known by us. The flavors of the wine we drink during Holy Communion remind us of many things: the suffering of Christ, the longing of the Lord for his return, and the promises of God that are still waiting to be fulfilled.

And that will be something I hope to treasure every time I obey the command "to do this in remembrance of Me."

Full-Circle

Leif and I were planning another trip to Portland, and Lynne invited us to return to the farm to catch up. Though it had only been a short while, the visit to Lynne's home brought back warm memories of our time together and gave me a chance to reflect on my travels.

The insights and truths I'd discovered while scouting the divine allowed me to realize something big about myself: my view of God is fractured. The Scriptures describe us as seeing in a mirror dimly, but I don't feel like my mirror is dark as much as it is shattered. I see shards of truth but grapple to understand how they fit together.

My broken understanding of God makes me feel helpless. In my heart and mind, I know that God is abundantly kind. I know he is the purest definition of wisdom and the designer of love. On occasion, I have found myself captivated by his beauty, but more often than not I am confused by his mystery. To say the least, our incomprehensible God is difficult for me to grasp.

I struggle to reconcile what I know of God and what I see in our world. God demands justice, yet on countless occasions I see injustice prevail. God's presence breathes life and multiplies; yet I am confronted by unexplainable death and loss on the evening news. God invites all to repentance, yet some of my closest friends and family have never responded. Bad things happen to good people, and good things happen to bad people, and I don't know which is more difficult to wrap my mind around.

The shards of my broken perspective cut painfully.

The questions I have asked many times before—*Why God? How long? When is it enough?*—surface once again.

Yet as I reflect on my time with the wine, wool, and wild honey, some of the pieces in my broken understanding of God come together for the first time. In each setting I was able to recognize something new about God and his kingdom.

In the eyes of the shepherd and in the presence of the sheep, I gained a new appreciation of God. I watched a shepherd who truly loved her sheep—it was evident in the way she spoke to and about them. Whether feeding her animals by hand, changing their bandages, administering medicine, or keeping a watchful eye, her love was on constant display. It reignited my own trust in God's love for each of us—a love that is tangible, practical, and unending. Even Lynne's acts of punishment among the sheep were acts of love and mercy. From this perspective, some of the seemingly opposite attributes of God, like discipline and grace, begin to make sense.

My time with the farmer revealed that some of the difficulty I have in understanding God is related to not being able to grasp his timing. When things don't come together like I anticipate or expect, I fret about what could have been. In those moments, the gap between the promises of God and the fulfillment of those promises grows wider. Yet my time in the fields revealed that everything has its season. Though I may not enjoy the time period I am currently in, it will pass. Another will come. And whether I like it or not, another will come after that. In my life, I will experience times of joy, of sorrow, of anticipation, and of failed expectations—but I cling to the fact that in all the many seasons, my constant source of joy and peace is rooted in someone much wiser than I.

My time with the beekeeper and his bees opened my eyes to see that God is at work in more ways than I could ever imagine. In the hive, every bee has a purpose. The queen lays eggs. The drones fertilize the queen. The harvesters gather nectar. In a hive of tens of thousands, it's impossible for a single bee to recognize the magnitude of all that's happening to make a drop of honey, let alone what the world would look like if bees didn't pollinate. In the same way, it's impossible for me to fully grasp how much God is accomplishing through his people (including me) and the church. Though I get glimpses, God alone knows the full story, and maybe, just maybe, I'm learning to be okay with that.

My time with the vintner taught me something about the paradox of pruning that deep down I didn't really want to know: to grow, we must be cut back. Just as the vine cannot produce quality grapes year-round, neither can we expect to be fruitful all day, every day. Though painful, careful pruning is one of God's greatest acts of love. Through the vintner I discovered God as the keeper of the vine—one who has protected and girdled me so that I can bear the fruit that he has created and nurtured me to produce.

On this journey I've been blessed by gifts—a bag of wool from the shepherd, freshly canned tomatoes from the farmer's family, a golden jar of honey from the beekeeper, a bottle of fine red wine from the vintner. My heart fills with gratitude for all these people who gave out of their experiences, lives, and wisdom. As a pilgrim on the road, I recognize that I have a responsibility to pass on what I've learned.

The shepherd, the farmer, the beekeeper, and the vintner were all passionate about what they did. Their work wasn't a matter of duty as much as it was an act of delight. They worked hard, tackling tough issues and difficult days. But when they spoke about what they did, each of them had the unmistakable tone of love in their voice.

That is the underlying tone that I have been longing to hear in God's voice. An inflection that reminds me that in the angst, bitterness, and imperfection of the world as I know it, in everything that appears to be broken, God is still in love with his creation.

Why is that so important?

Because deep down inside, the consistent and unmistakable tone of God's love keeps me going. It makes me want to love him and others more. It infuses me with the hope that despite all that is shattered in me, my perspective, and the world around me, God is still good. A good and loving God is committed to redemption and restoration—not just in my own life, but in our world.

At times I'm tempted to think that I live in a world where my actions are merely my own. These keepers of the land and animals remind me that we live in a universe where we are all responsible for our choices and the effects they have on others. The choices of everyone I spent time with could be clearly seen in the health of their animals or produce of their fields. The journey of following Jesus will always be decided in the most basic of life choices, and the choices I make today will yield a harvest. Each decision matters.

Back in Oregon, I found myself sitting with Lynne in the same rocking chair that I had enjoyed months before. The fire crackled as we caught up on life and our latest travels. Lynne invited me out to the fields to see the sheep. Because they had grown so much, the lambs were unrecognizable to me—except for Swan, still the smallest of them all.

The flock surrounded us, their woolly bodies pressed up against us in hopes of a savory treat.

"Do you recognize that one?" Lynne asked.

I stared at the amber sheep. She didn't look familiar at all.

"That's Piaget," Lynne said.

I couldn't believe my eyes. The sheep that had worn a homemade diaper and teetered between life and death for weeks looked vibrant and alive.

"She wasn't that color before," I protested.

Lynne explained that the medicine she had taken acted like chemotherapy. Her gray wool had grown back brown.

"She looks great!" I said.

"She sure does," Lynne said proudly.

If Lynne went to such great lengths to save a sick ewe like Piaget, how much further will God go to save us? We live in a world seared by sickness, accidents, and pain, yet God, like Lynne with Piaget, stays beside us through our darkest nights because he can see the far-off light.

After spending time with the flock, Tom, Leif, Lynne, and I enjoyed a delicious dinner together. "Since our conversation, have you found yourself more attuned to spiritual ideas regarding sheep?" I asked.

"Absolutely," Lynne replied. "I just wish I could spend more time with all the Scriptures you showed me."

I thought about the dozens of Scriptures I had discussed with Lynne and how together they revealed so much about God. From the prophet who paints a rich portrait of God as a tender shepherd caring for his people to Isaiah telling us that in heaven we will find lambs resting alongside wolves in the age to come, I had found my hope and faith strengthened. Maybe I wasn't the only one.

"All those Bible verses blew me away," Lynne added. "I keep having thoughts about them."

"Me too," I said.

I glanced in the direction of the barn, knowing that the sheep were gathered safely inside. The lambs were nestled in pockets of hay next to their mother ewes. Together, they enjoyed the warmth and safety of the surrounding flock under the gentle care of a good shepherd.

Hidden Bonus Tracks

Scouting the Divine
Study & Discussion

It's no secret that I love the Bible. I believe that it's the most life-transforming book that we can ever read, and I'm passionate about introducing it to people in ways that are practical, accessible, and enjoyable. What you've just read has been a heartfelt attempt to make the Bible come alive in a fresh and innovative way. My hope is that in our time together you heard God speak to you and were challenged in your own spiritual journey. I've been praying that through these pages you've felt a renewed hunger to know God and his Word. Normally, at the end of my books I provide a series of discussion questions, but the material covered in this book only scratches the surface of all I discovered on my journey.

That's why I've partnered with Lifeway to develop a six-week *Scouting the Divine* video series. This will allow you and a group of your friends to dig deeper into the story and Scripture. I would highly encourage you to consider using this kit as the basis for your personal study, small groups, Bible studies, and book clubs. Visit *www.margaretfeinberg.com* to learn more.

In the meantime, here are a few questions that may come in handy as you discuss the book:

1. What concept, phrase, or story was the most compelling to you?

2. What concept, phrase, or idea did you disagree with?

3. What did you learn about God or his Word through *Scouting the Divine?*

Behind the Scenes

Wonderment

11 overflowing with life: I want to be clear that aha! moments within Scripture are often rare, and it is essential that we read God's Word faithfully whether or not we have an aha! moment. Reading the Scripture is a good, valuable, and essential part of the Christian life. And sometimes aha! moments are like the sugar that we crave and long for and God even promises, but we must remember that character and growth and faithfulness increase when we persevere in our study and pursuit of knowing God when there are no aha! moments to be found.

12 never grasped before: Some of the names and details of this book have been changed in order to respect the privacy of individuals.

Part I: The Good Shepherd

15 any other state: Alaskans consume more ice cream per capita (depending on how you shuffle the numbers—remember that Alaska has a whole lot of visitors eating cones during the summer). *http:// icecreamjournal.turkeyhill.com/index.php/2008/12/23/12-days-of-ice -cream-day-9-which-state-eats-the-most-ice-cream/*.

21 ordered three: In 1992, when Lynne began looking for Shetland sheep, they were hard to find, almost considered a rare breed. That's why she had to mail order sheep. Now they are abundant throughout the United States. All registered farms receive a number. Lynne is the eightieth in the country. Now there are close to two thousand registered farms.

24 I wondered: I was watching a process—a shepherd calling sheep—that had been repeated for millennia. In the Middle East, even in modern times, the shepherd's voice is essential to the flock's survival. As different children within a family assume the role of shepherding their family's flock, they must be introduced to the flock over time. On rare occasions, a family may find itself in a situation where the transition between shepherds has not taken place and the sheep can't or won't learn from a new voice. In these situations, families sometimes have to destroy the entire flock.

25 sheep is missing: Luke 15:3–7.

28 stink eye: To truly appreciate "the stink eye," you'll need to watch the movie *Juno*.

38 the visitor: 2 Samuel 12:1–4.

38 shepherd-king's memory: 1 Chronicles 17:7–8; 2 Samuel 18:6.

40 from the field: Genesis 4:2–5.

40 their flocks: Genesis 13:5–6.

40 among other gifts: Genesis 12:14–16; also, at this point, Abram's name had not been changed to Abraham.

41 "The Lord Will Provide": Genesis 22:13–14; John H. Walton, *The NIV Application Commentary: Genesis* (Grand Rapids: Zondervan, 2001), 510.

41 a shepherd: Exodus 2:15–22. The Egyptians despised shepherds for a variety of reasons, many of them obvious, including the fact that they were dirty, smelly, and even given to the reputation of being thieves.

41 God's people: Exodus 3–4:18.

41 value of their sheep: Exodus 10:24–25.

41 without yeast: Exodus 12:1–13.

42 shepherd-turned-prophet: Hosea 4:16; Jeremiah 3:14–15; Ezekiel 34; Micah 2:12–13; Nahum 3:18; Zechariah 10:3; Amos 1:1.

42 "shepherd" Israel: Micah 5:2–4; Matthew 2:6.

42 Jesus' birth: Luke 2:8–18.

42 "Lamb of God": John 1:35–36.

46 a real sacrifice: According to Lynne, everyone wants the first shearing, but not many people get one because shepherds usually hold back the best first shearing for themselves. "Only if we have a very big flock and have more first shearings than we can personally use do we sell first shearings," she explained, "and even then we sell those particular shearings for a high price."

48   (Numbers 27:16–17): This comparison to being sheep without a shepherd is found throughout the Bible in passages like 1 Kings 22:17.

48   on the crowds: 2 Chronicles 18:16; Isaiah 13:14; Mark 6:34.

50   "without a shepherd": Matthew 9:36.

51   propensity to wander: www.followtherabbi.com/Brix?pageID=1783.

53   rule over Israel: I heart Eugene Peterson, author of *The Message*.

54   abundant flocks: Genesis 26:14.

54   falls in love: Genesis 29:2–11.

57   "midst of predators": Michael J. Wilkins, *The NIV Application Commentary: Matthew* (Grand Rapids: Zondervan, 2004), 391–92.

58   (Luke 19): By the way, the NASB spells this man's name "Zaccheus," rather than "Zacchaeus."

63   "Shepherd of Israel": Psalm 80:1; Ezekiel 34:11–16.

64   "Shepherd of the sheep": Hebrews 13:20.

64   "Guardian of your souls": 1 Peter 2:24–25.

64   "the Chief Shepherd": 1 Peter 5:4.

Part II: The Harvest

71   Check it out for yourself: www.urbandictionary.com/define.php?term=wenis.

75   someone else: Luke 12:13–21.

77   fruitful crop: Mark 4:1–20.

79   the firstfruits of their produce: Deuteronomy 26:1–11.

80   animal to suffer: Ralph Gower, *The New Manners and Customs of Bible Times* (Chicago: Moody, 1987), 88–9.

81   avoid judging each other: Matthew 7:1–5.

81   works of the flesh: Galatians 5:16–24.

82   from which we come: The account of creation in Genesis is a work of literary beauty. A rich parallelism is found between the first three days and the last three days of creation. Days one and four, two and five, and three and six are all similar. For example, day three contains two parts (God dividing land and sky as well as creating vegetation) and day six contains two parts (God creating animals and people). I think I could study the two chapters of Genesis for a lifetime and never grasp all the depth or meaning.

83 cares for us: *The Green Bible* (San Francisco: HarperOne), 1–28.

83 (Deuteronomy 5:16): *The Green Bible* (San Francisco: HarperOne), 1–60.

84 Lord blesses him: Genesis 26:12.

84 kind of produce: Psalm 144:13.

84 God's law: Isaiah 17:11; Jeremiah 8:20.

84 teaching and instruction: 1 Samuel 12:17; Judges 6:4–5; Job 31:12; Amos 4:7.

84 severe harvest losses: 2 Samuel 21:1.

85 day and night: Genesis 8:22.

85 Feast of Booths: Exodus 23:16.

85 to the priests: Leviticus 23:9–14.

85 door to a new life: Leviticus 19:9; 23:22.

86 sharp sickle: Revelation 14:17–20.

88 God's kingdom: Luke 9:61–62.

88 not looking back: Ralph Gower, *The New Manners and Customs of Bible Times* (Chicago: Moody, 1987), 90–91.

89 in the wilderness: Numbers 21:8–9.

89 people to himself: John 12:32.

89 perfecter of faith: Hebrews 12:2.

90 I asked: Matthew 3:12.

92 all circumstances: Philippians 4:11–13.

93 acts shamefully: Proverbs 10:5.

94 in need: Miriam Feinberg Vamosh, *Daily Life at the Time of Jesus* (Nashville: Abingdon, 2001), 46.

94 send out workers: Matthew 9:37–38.

94 called to serve: Matthew 10:1–15.

95 "'ought to have done'": Luke 17:10.

100 are furious: Genesis 37:5–8.

102 harvest time: Exodus 34:21.

107 fertility god of Egypt: Genesis 45:6–7.

Part III: The Land of Milk and Honey

125   various spiritual gifts: Ephesians 4:11–13.

127   all pollination: In addition to drinking nectar from flowers, bees also collect pollen on their hind legs in a concave area known as a pollen basket. They store the pollen in the hive as a protein source that is needed when rearing the brood. To learn more, check out *www .honey.com/downloads/storyofhoneyweb.pdf*.

131   provides the honey: Psalm 81:16; Ezekiel 16:19.

131   burning bush: Exodus 3:8.

131   hiding from Saul: 2 Samuel 17:26–29.

131   her travels: 1 Kings 14:3.

132   the tithe: 2 Chronicles 31:4–6.

132   ancient practice: *www.sciencenews.org/view/generic/id/36043 /title/Honey_of_a_discovery*.

Also, for a great two-minute video that highlights "The Beehives of Tel Rehov," check out *www.sourceflix.com/vid_rehov.htm*.

132   "a little": Genesis 43:11.

132   "milk and honey": Exodus 3:8.

132   overflowed with provision: The Hebrew word used for honey, which appears more than fifty times in the Old Testament, has been translated as "bee's honey" or "syrup." In antiquity, natural sugars were produced by fruits such as dates or apricots as well as the honey produced by bees. The idea that bees had been domesticated to some level is conveyed in 2 Chronicles 31:5, regarding the firstfruit offerings. For more details, check out: Merrill C. Tenney, ed., *The Zondervan Pictorial Encyclopedia of the Bible*, vol. 3 (Grand Rapids: Zondervan, 1975), 196.

133   wafers with honey: Exodus 16:31.

134   posture relaxed: All those I interviewed were hesitant when I began talking about specific passages in the Bible, hesitant that because they weren't theologians or professors of religious studies, they didn't have anything to contribute to the conversation. While I think we have to be wise and careful about interpreting Scripture, I was saddened that those I interviewed felt like they had to be experts to engage in a thoughtful discussion of God's Word instead of recognizing that we were both learning together.

134   a single day: *www.honey.com.*

138   healing to the bones: Proverbs 16:24.

138   "helps with allergies": This book does not endorse the use of honey for any medical remedy. Please consult a professional before using honey for any medicinal or health reasons.

138   remain in place: "Honey in the Treatment of Wounds and Burns," Molan PC. "Potential of honey in the treatment of wounds and burns." *American Journal of Clinical Dermatology* 2001; 2(1):13–19 and *http://www.honey.com/downloads/HoneyAndWellness.pdf.*

139   curds and honey: Isaiah 7:15.

139   vines devastated: Isaiah 7:15–22.

139   people to embrace: Matthew 3:4; 2 Kings 1:8.

142   remains the same: 1 Corinthians 12:1–12.

Part IV: The Vine

145   except for Cathleen: Cathleen Falsani is a gifted journalist, writer, and friend. If you have not read her book, *Sin Boldly: A Field Guide to Grace*, I highly recommend it!

154   his Father: Simon J. Kistemaker, *The Miracles: Exploring the Mystery of Jesus' Divine Works* (Grand Rapids: Baker, 2006), 13–18, and Gary Burge, *The NIV Application Commentary: John* (Grand Rapids: Zondervan, 2000), 88–93.

161   plant vineyards: Numbers 16:13–14; Deuteronomy 8:7–9.

161   an angel: Numbers 22:23–25.

162   God's vineyard: Isaiah 5:1–2.

162   scarcity of fruit: Isaiah 5:2.

162   fruit as rotting: Hosea 10:1.

162   "a foreign vine": Jeremiah 2:21.

162   God's judgment: Jeremiah 5:10; Hosea 2:12; Amos 4:9.

162   a new vineyard: Isaiah 5:5–7.

162   enjoy the fruit: Deuteronomy 28:30, 39.

162   of their sin: Zephaniah 1:13.

163 forbids drunkenness: Ephesians 5:17–18.

163 God's people: Amos 9:14.

163 own grandsons: Genesis 9:20–27.

163 decisions that come with it: Genesis 19:30–38; 2 Samuel 13:28; 1 Kings 20:16; 2 Samuel 11:13; Isaiah 5:22; Proverbs 23:29–35.

164 Joseph interpreted: Genesis 40:8–14.

167 broken down: Proverbs 24:30–31.

168 plant a vineyard: Proverbs 31:16–17.

168 avoiding strong drink: Proverbs 23.

169 planted vineyards: Ecclesiastes 2:4.

172 wine and wineskins: Matthew 9:14–17; Luke 5:37–39.

177 "Pella" in calligraphy: To learn more about Kristof's work and boutique wine, visit *www.pellawine.com.*

178 Passover celebration: The four cups of the Passover celebration are representative of the four "I wills" in Exodus 6:6–7. These include: The Cup of Sanctification—"I will bring you out from under the burdens of the Egyptians"; The Cup of Judgment or Deliverance—"I will deliver you from their bondage"; The Cup of Redemption—"I will also redeem you with an outstretched arm"; and The Cup of Praise or Restoration—"I will take you for My people, and I will be your God."

179 "my own people": Michael J. Wilkins, *The NIV Application Commentary: Matthew* (Grand Rapids: Zondervan, 2004), 838–9.

Full-Circle

181 it is shattered: 1 Corinthians 13:12.

185 for his people: Isaiah 40:10–12.

186 age to come: Isaiah 11:6.

Scouting the Divine Soundtrack

Part I: The Good Shepherd

Nickelback, "If Today Was Your Last Day," *Dark Horse*
U2, "White as Snow," *No Line On The Horizon*
Kim Walker, "How He Loves," *We Cry Out*
Corinne Bailey Rae, "Put Your Records On," *Corinne Bailey Rae*

Part II: The Harvest

Coldplay, "Strawberry Swing," *Vida la Vida*
Kings of Leon, "Use Somebody," *Because of the Times*
Josh Wilson, "Savior, Please," *Trying to Fit the Ocean in a Cup*
Lady Antebellum, "Never Alone," feat. Jim
    Brickman, *Lady Antebellum*

Part III: The Land of Milk and Honey

Leif Sunde, "Trust in Me," *Undone* (available on iTunes)
Shinedown, "Second Chance," *The Sound of Madness*
Matchbox Twenty, "How Far We've Come," *Exile on Mainstream*
Phil Wickham, "I Will Wait for You There," (available on iTunes)

Part IV: The Vine

Dave Matthews Band, "Funny the Way It Is,"
    Big Whiskey and the Groogrux King
Addison Road, "Hope Now," *Addison Road*
Chris Tomlin, "I Will Rise," *Hello Love*
Annie Brooks, "It Is Love," *When the*
    Kings and Queens Have Gone

Add your own suggestions at www.margaretfeinberg.com

Abundant Props

Leif O.	Carol R.
Lynne & Tom D.	Marty R.
Leonard H.	Angela S.
Gary M.	Becky P.
Kristof A.	Curt D.
Dave T.	Kelly J.
Jana R.	Tom D.
Tim W.	Brad H.
Jonathan M.	Mark B.
Tracee H.	Chris F.
Todd L.	Hershey O.
Scot M.	Leslie & Dale M.
Jessica R.	Marjane & Bill F.

Meet the Author

Margaret Feinberg is a popular Bible teacher and speaker at churches and leading conferences such as Catalyst and Women of Joy. Her books and Bible studies, including *Taste and See*, *Scouting the Divine*, *Fight Back with Joy*, *Wonderstruck*, and *The Sacred Echo*, have sold more than a million copies combined and received critical acclaim and extensive national media coverage from CNN, the Associated Press, *USA Today*, the *Los Angeles Times*, the *Washington Post*, and many others.

She was named one of the 50 women most shaping culture and the church today by *Christianity Today*. Margaret lives in Park City, Utah, with her husband Leif who serves as a local pastor, and their superpup, Hershey.

One of her greatest joys is hearing from her readers. Go ahead, find her on Facebook, Twitter, and Instagram (@mafeinberg), or check out her website at margaretfeinberg.com.

Free
Gifts

I'm so delighted that we have the opportunity to Scout the Divine together. In appreciation and celebration, I've put together some free gifts for you—including fun invitations, posts, and even recipes. I'd love to send downloads to you for your surprise and delight. Simply email us at:

hello@margaretfeinberg.com

New Video Study for Your Church or Small Group

If you've enjoyed this book, now you can go deeper with the companion video Bible study!

In this six-session study, Margaret Feinberg helps you apply the principles of *Scouting the Divine* to your life. The study guide includes video notes, group discussion questions, and personal study and reflection materials for in-between sessions.

To order visit MargaretFeinbergStore.com

Join your friend, Margaret Feinberg, for the hap-hap-happiest half-hour of your week on The Joycast. Available on iTunes, Spotify, and most podcast hosts—as well as at margaretfeinberg.com.

Listen & Subscribe Today!

GOD IS A FOODIE

WHO WANTS TO TRANSFORM YOUR SUPPER INTO SACRAMENT.

One of America's most beloved teachers and writers, Margaret Feinberg, takes you on a culinary exploration of Scripture. You'll learn fresh biblical discoveries as she wanders a California fig farm, bakes fresh matzo at Yale University, descends 400 feet into a salt mine, visits a remote island in Croatia to harvest olives, and studies under a butcher known as "the meat apostle."

With each visit, Margaret asks, "How do you read these Scriptures, not as theologians, but in light of what you do every day?" Their answers will forever change the way you read the Bible—and approach every meal.

ORDER THE 6-SESSION DVD BIBLE STUDY TODAY!

Printed in the USA
CPSIA information can be obtained
at www.ICGtesting.com
JSHW032017240624
65293JS00011B/112